CW01456923

Artificial Intelligence Explained

The Complete Beginner's Guide -
50 Essential Answers by AI, Clarified for Humans

PUBLISHED BY: Stephen D. Carver

Copyright © 2025
All rights reserved.

No part of this publication may be reproduced, distributed, or trans-mitted in any form or by any means, including photocopying, recording, or other electronic or mechanical methods, without the prior written per-mission of the publisher, except in the case of brief quotations used in reviews, articles, or educational purposes permitted by copyright law.

This book is intended for informational and educational purposes only. While every effort has been made to ensure accuracy, the author and publisher make no representations or warranties with respect to the completeness or accuracy of the contents and specifically disclaim any implied warranties of merchantability or fitness for a particular purpose. The author and publisher shall not be liable for any damages arising from the use of this book

Contents

Introduction

Artificial intelligence. Two words that seem to appear everywhere these days. From the news to your workplace, from the apps on your phone to debates in politics and philosophy, AI has become the buzzword of the decade. Depending on who you ask, it's either a magical tool that will solve humanity's toughest problems or a dangerous technology that could put us all out of work, or worse.

But if we take a step back and ask a simple question - what actually is AI? - the answers suddenly get vague. Some describe it as machines "thinking like humans". Others call it "automation on steroids". Some even confuse it with robots or science fiction characters. The truth is, artificial intelligence is many things at once: a science, a set of tools, a way of solving problems, and increasingly, a force shaping our daily lives in ways both subtle and dramatic.

That's where this book comes in. *Artificial Intelligence Explained* is exactly what the title promises: an exploration of artificial intelligence, written with the help of artificial intelligence itself. It's a dialogue - fifty questions and fifty answers, plus a bonus chapter on generative AI - that brings together human curiosity and machine-generated explanations. My role, as the human author, is to ask the right questions, provide context, and add commentary that makes these answers approachable, relevant, and sometimes even a little fun.

Why another book on AI?

There are plenty of books, articles, and videos about artificial intelligence. Some are highly technical, aimed at researchers or engineers. Others are sensational, promising either utopia or doom. What's missing, however, is a guide that balances clarity with accuracy: something you can read without a computer science degree but that still respects your intelligence.

This book aims to be that guide. You won't find long equations or programming tutorials here, but you also won't find shallow hype. Instead, you'll discover clear explanations of key ideas, practical examples, and thoughtful reflections on what AI means for us as individuals, professionals, and members of society.

Whether you're a student curious about the future of work, a manager wondering how AI might affect your industry, or simply someone who keeps hearing about "neural networks" and "large language models" and wants to finally understand what they are, this book is for you.

Why structure it as questions and answers?

AI itself thrives on questions. You ask, and it answers. That's how many of us first encounter it: typing a query into a chatbot, giving a command to a voice assistant, or searching for information online. Structuring the book as 50 questions and answers mirrors this natural interaction. It makes the material approachable: instead of overwhelming you with abstract chapters, we focus on curiosity.

Each question is one that real people ask. Some are basic: *"What is AI, really?"*. Others are deeper: *"Is AI creative?"*, *"Does AI understand, or just predict?"*, *"Will AI take over all jobs?"*. Still others are philosophical: *"Is AI conscious?"* or *"What are the biggest risks of AI in the future?"*. By exploring these questions step by step, we move from the basics of how AI works to the complex debates shaping its future.

And here's the twist: the answers come from AI itself. This doesn't mean I simply let the machine write the book and left it at that. Instead, I treated AI as a collaborator. For each question, the AI provides a structured, informative answer. Then I, as the human guide, add commentary - connecting the dots, giving real-world examples, highlighting what's missing, and sometimes poking fun at the machine's "voice".

The result is a unique hybrid: explanations that are at once technical and human, precise and conversational.

Why let AI explain itself?

Some readers might wonder: isn't it strange to let AI "explain itself"? Doesn't that create bias or circular reasoning? It's a fair concern. After all, AI doesn't "know" things the way humans do. It doesn't have awareness or beliefs. It generates answers based on patterns in data.

But that's precisely what makes this experiment valuable. By letting AI answer, we see both its strengths and its limitations. We see how it frames knowledge, where it's clear, and where it oversimplifies. We learn not just *about AI* but also *from AI*. My commentary is there to fill in the gaps, to push back when needed, and to make sure the answers remain grounded in reality.

Think of it this way: if you want to understand a foreign language, you don't just study grammar - you listen to native speakers. If you want to understand AI, it makes sense to "listen" to AI itself, while keeping a critical human perspective.

A journey for everyone

Another important point: this book is for everyone. You don't need to be a programmer, a mathematician, or a philosopher. You just need curiosity. If you can follow a conversation, you can follow this book.

At the same time, I haven't shied away from depth. You'll encounter terms like "neural networks", "training data", "bias", and "large language models". But don't worry: each will be explained clearly, with analogies, examples, and metaphors. My goal is to leave you smarter and more confident, not more confused.

By the end, you won't just know what AI *is* but, instead, you'll have a sense of how it works, why it matters, what its risks are, and how it might shape the decades to come.

A word about hype and fear

Before we begin, it's worth addressing the elephant in the room: AI is surrounded by both hype and fear. On one hand, we hear promises of machines that will cure diseases, solve climate change, and unlock endless productivity. On the other hand, we hear warnings of mass unemployment, social disruption, and even superintelligent machines that could one day surpass us.

This book won't give you extreme answers. Instead, it will offer balanced perspectives. AI is powerful, yes. It is changing the world, yes. But it is not magic. It's built by humans, trained on data from humans, and limited by human choices. Understanding these realities is the first step toward using AI wisely, whether in your personal life or your profession.

How to read this book

You can read the book straight through, from Question 1 to Question 50, watching the story of AI unfold from basics to future visions. Or you can dip into it, picking up the questions that matter most to you. Each Q&A stands alone, but together they form a complete picture.

My suggestion? Start at the beginning, especially if you're new to the field. Even simple questions contain shades you might not expect, and later chapters build on those foundations.

The future is now

One final thought before we dive in: AI is not just a topic of the future. It's already here, shaping search engines, social media, healthcare, finance, entertainment, and more. Every time you unlock your phone with your face, get a movie recommendation, or use autocorrect, AI is quietly at work. Understanding it isn't optional anymore: it's essential. And the good news is, you don't need to be an engineer to grasp the basics. By the end of this book, you'll be equipped not only to understand what AI is but also to think critically about its role in your life and society.

So, let's get started. Fifty questions, fifty answers, and one bonus chapter. Curiosity meets computation. Human meets machine.

Welcome to *Artificial Intelligence Explained.*

Author's Note

When I first encountered artificial intelligence, I was both fascinated and overwhelmed. On one hand, the technology seemed magical: machines that could write, predict, or even compose music. On the other, the discussions around AI were often either too technical or filled with alarmist hype. I wanted something different: a clear, honest, and accessible explanation that anyone could understand.

This book is the result of that curiosity. I asked questions that I, and countless others, had about AI, from the basics to the more complex ideas shaping our future. Then, I turned to AI itself to answer them. But I didn't stop there. I wanted to make sure the answers were not only accurate but meaningful, so I added commentary, examples, and insights to guide readers through the concepts.

Writing this book has been a journey of discovery, learning, and sometimes even surprise. AI, as I quickly realized, is both a tool and a mirror: it reflects our intelligence, our creativity, and even our biases. By understanding AI, we also learn more about ourselves and the choices we face in a world increasingly shaped by technology.

My hope is that this book will make AI approachable, informative, and even a little fun. Whether you are reading it to understand your work, your studies, or simply your curiosity about the world, I want you to finish with confidence, a clear sense of what AI is, how it works, and why it matters.

Thank you for joining me on this journey. I can't wait to explore these fifty questions, and the bonus chapter, with you, and I hope you'll find the answers as enlightening and thought-provoking as I have.

- Stephen D. Carver

Chapter 1: Understanding AI Basics

Every conversation about AI must start with the basics: what it is, what it isn't, and why it matters. This chapter clears up the myths and gives us the foundation to build on.

Q1: What is artificial intelligence, really?

AI Answer

Artificial intelligence (AI) is a branch of computer science focused on creating systems that can perform tasks we usually associate with human intelligence. These tasks range from recognizing speech and understanding language to analyzing images, solving problems, and making decisions. At its core, AI is about designing machines that can learn from data, adapt to new situations, and behave in ways that appear intelligent.

The idea of AI isn't new. The term was first introduced in 1956 at a workshop at Dartmouth College, where researchers dreamed of machines that could "think". Progress was slow at first, limited by weak computing power and small datasets. For decades, enthusiasm came in waves, followed by "AI winters" when results failed to match the hype.

Real progress came with machine learning, which shifted the approach from programming strict rules to training systems on examples. Instead of coding thousands of conditions, engineers fed algorithms with data and let them detect patterns. Later, in the 2010s, deep learning accelerated this progress. By stacking many layers of artificial "neurons", computers could automatically spot features in data, from simple shapes in photos to subtle phrases in language. Deep learning made AI useful at scale, powering, voice assistants, search engines and even game-playing systems that outperformed world champions.

Today, the most visible form of AI is generative AI. Unlike earlier tools that classified or predicted, generative systems create new content: essays, code, art, or even music. Tools like ChatGPT and DALL·E brought AI into everyday life because anyone can type a prompt and get an original response. While the results often feel magical, underneath they are still pattern recognition, sophisticated guesses based on probabilities.

It's also worth stressing what AI is *not*. It doesn't have consciousness, emotions, or intent. It doesn't "think" as we do. Instead, it processes data at massive scale, identifying patterns that would be impossible for humans to detect alone.

So, what is AI really? It's best understood as a tool of amplification. Just as the printing press amplified how we share ideas, AI amplifies how we process and generate information. It doesn't replace human intelligence, but it extends it, helping us work faster, smarter, and at a scale we could never reach on our own.

Human Commentary

When I first heard about artificial intelligence, I pictured robots plotting world domination. The truth turned out to be far less dramatic and much closer to home. Before I ever used ChatGPT, I was already using AI without realizing it: my calendar app suggested meeting times, my phone mapped the fastest way through traffic, and streaming apps queued up songs I might like. AI wasn't in the future, it was in my pocket.

The real shift came when AI became visible. Instead of silently shaping my inbox or playlists, it started answering me directly. Writing this book with AI's help still feels strange. On the one hand, it's a powerful assistant: I can draft market analysis, brainstorm slides, or even ask for dinner recipes. On the other, it's unsettling, because the conversation feels human even though I know it isn't.

If I had to explain AI over coffee, I'd say this: imagine a super-intern who has read every encyclopedia, watched every YouTube video, and memorized every Wikipedia page. He can draft an email or suggest a recipe instantly. But he doesn't know what heartbreak feels like, he's never laughed at an inside joke, and he'll never taste your grandmother's pasta sauce.

That's the line: AI is brilliant, but not human.

Q2: How does AI learn from data?

AI Answer

One of the most important things about AI is how it learns: not by memorizing like a student cramming facts, but by training on data until it recognizes patterns, which means feeding it large amounts of data and letting it adjust its internal settings until it can make accurate predictions. A useful way to picture this is to imagine teaching children. You show them dozens of pictures of animals, pointing and saying "cat" or "dog". Over time, they notice recurring features (whiskers, tails, floppy ears) and can correctly identify new animals they've never seen. AI does something similar, except instead of intuition it relies on mathematics.

At the core of training are weights, numerical values that determine how important certain features are when making a decision. If an AI is learning to recognize cats, it might give "pointy ears" a high weight, while "fur color" gets a low one. When the system makes a mistake, an algorithm adjusts these weights slightly. After millions of corrections, the model becomes skilled at recognizing cats or, more broadly, whatever task it was trained for.

There are several ways AI can learn:

- **Supervised learning:** the AI is trained on labeled data ("this is a cat, this is not"). It's used in handwriting recognition for bank checks, airport security screening, and credit card fraud detection;

- **Unsupervised learning:** data has no labels, and the AI must find hidden patterns, such as grouping customers by shopping behavior;
- **Reinforcement learning:** the AI learns by trial and error, receiving rewards for good outcomes. This method trained systems such as AlphaGo, which defeated world champions at the game of Go.

In the past, humans had to carefully design "features", telling the system to measure things like ear shape or nose size. Deep learning changed that. Modern neural networks automatically discover which features matter, which is why they can detect fraud in millions of transactions or identify unusual patterns in financial markets.

However, learning is only as good as the data provided. Biased or incomplete datasets lead to biased AI. For instance, if a medical system only sees examples from one demographic group, it may fail to diagnose patients from others. The old saying "garbage in, garbage out" applies perfectly here.

Ultimately, AI's strength is practice at scale. What takes humans months or years to learn, an AI can compress into hours of training, provided it has enough good data to work with.

Human Commentary

A friend once asked me to explain AI training, and I said: "Think of it as homework, endless homework". She laughed, but the comparison works. Just like a student improves through practice, AI gets better by grinding through exercises, repeatedly, until patterns sink in.

In my own career, I've lived through a version of this. My first sales calls were clumsy: I misread client signals, rambled too much, and sometimes missed the real question entirely. But after dozens of conversations, I started to notice patterns - a certain hesitation that meant "I'm not convinced", or a quick nod that meant "you're on the right track". Over time, I got better. That's learning. The difference is that AI does the same process at warp speed, absorbing millions of "calls" in hours instead of months.

The catch is that AI doesn't develop intuition. I can glance at a client's body language and sense curiosity or boredom. An algorithm can't - not yet. It only sees numbers and probabilities. That's why AI feels so powerful and so limited at the same time: brilliant at repetition, but blind to context.

In short, AI is the ultimate student. It never sleeps, never complains, and never forgets. But it still needs a teacher.

Q3: What's the difference between AI, machine learning, and deep learning?

AI Answer

People often use the terms AI, machine learning, and deep learning interchangeably - but they're not the same. To understand the relationship, it helps to imagine a set of nested circles: AI is the broadest, ML sits inside AI, and DL is a special case of ML.

Artificial Intelligence (AI) is the umbrella concept. It refers to any system built to perform tasks we associate with human intelligence - problem-solving, reasoning, language understanding, decision-making. Early AI in the 1950s and 1960s relied on rigid rules: "if the user says X, then respond with Y". These programs worked in narrow contexts but collapsed in messy real-world situations.

Machine Learning (ML) later made AI more adaptable. Instead of coding every rule, engineers trained algorithms on data so the system could detect patterns. For example, a fraud detection model doesn't need rules for every possible case; it learns from thousands of examples labeled "fraudulent" or "legitimate". ML powers tools we use daily: predictive text, product recommendations, dynamic pricing.

Deep Learning (DL) is one family of ML methods that has proven especially powerful. Its strength lies in handling vast amounts of data and enabling breakthroughs in areas such as speech recognition, image tagging, and generative systems.

A healthcare analogy makes the difference clear. Rule-based AI might say, "if fever + rash, then measles". ML would scan thousands of patient histories to find patterns. DL can go further, analyzing scans or audio recordings to detect subtle markers that humans might miss.

To summarize:

AI = the broad goal of building intelligent systems.

ML = a way to achieve AI by training on data.

DL = powerful approach within ML, especially good with large and complex datasets.

Without ML and DL, AI would remain mostly theoretical. With them, it has become practical, scalable, and part of daily life.

Human Commentary

When people ask me about the difference between AI, ML, and DL, I usually avoid technical definitions and reach for metaphors. My favorite is Russian nesting dolls: AI is the biggest doll, ML sits inside it, and DL is the smallest but most intricate one at the core. Another version I've used in meetings is sports: AI is "sports", ML is "team sports", and DL is "basketball". Each one narrows the focus.

The distinction matters because in business conversations, these terms get blurred. I've sat in meetings where someone said, "We need AI to predict sales". What they really meant was machine learning, since it's about spotting patterns in past data. When people talk about AI-generated art or music, that's deep learning at work. Understanding the vocabulary helps cut through the hype.

On a personal note, the first time I realized the power of deep learning was when I saw an AI system generate images that looked hand-painted. It wasn't just "statistics" anymore; it was producing something creative, something surprising. That's when I understood why these layers inside layers mattered - because sometimes the smallest doll carries the biggest punch.

Q4: Can AI think like a human?

AI Answer

One of the most common - and most misunderstood - questions about AI is whether it "thinks" like a human. The short answer is no. AI does not have consciousness, self-awareness, or emotions. It doesn't form opinions or experience the world. What it does is simulate aspects of human reasoning so convincingly that it can *appear* to think.

Human thinking is multidimensional. We combine logic, intuition, culture, and lived experience. For instance, when someone says "break a leg", we don't imagine an accident; we recognize it as encouragement. Our interpretation relies on memory, social context, and emotion.

AI works differently. A large language model like ChatGPT doesn't understand idioms - it has simply learned, from countless examples, that "break a leg" often appears in theater-related contexts. It predicts words based on statistical patterns, not meaning.

That's why AI is called narrow intelligence. It can excel in specific domains, like playing complex video games, forecasting demand in supply chains, or managing energy grids, but it cannot transfer that knowledge elsewhere. A chess engine cannot suddenly diagnose an illness, just as a medical imaging model cannot switch to composing music.

Researchers sometimes talk about Artificial General Intelligence (AGI) - a system with broad, human-like reasoning skills. Some believe AGI might emerge this century; others argue it may be impossible. What we have today is powerful but limited AI.

This distinction matters because anthropomorphizing AI - treating it as if it thinks or feels - can be misleading. A chatbot may generate convincing answers, but it doesn't "believe" in them. A translation app doesn't know the meaning of the words it outputs. They are simulations of thought, not thought itself.

So, can AI think like a human? Not at all. It calculates. It predicts. It mimics. But the inner world - imagination, emotion, experience - remains uniquely human.

We'll return to this in Q36, where we explore a related but different question: not whether AI thinks like us, but whether it could ever become *smarter* than us.

Human Commentary

I once asked an AI, half-jokingly, "Do you like Italian food?". It politely explained that it didn't have taste buds but could suggest recipes. That moment stuck with me. Helpful? Yes. Hungry? Definitely not.

What fascinates me is how easy it is to forget this distinction. In business, I've heard colleagues say, "Let's see what the AI thinks about this market". But AI doesn't think. It doesn't hold beliefs or form opinions. It runs calculations and presents patterns in words that sound thoughtful.

The best metaphor I've found is this: AI is like a sophisticated echo chamber. It can reflect back our words in ways that sound insightful, even original. But it has no idea what those words mean. Humans, by contrast, can look at a painting and feel nostalgia, joy, or sadness. AI only sees pixels and probabilities.

That's both the beauty and the danger. AI can simulate intelligence so well that we project humanity onto it. But remembering the gap - between simulation and experience - is essential if we want to use it wisely.

Q5: Why is AI suddenly everywhere now?

AI Answer

AI may feel like it appeared overnight, but its current popularity is the result of decades of gradual progress that suddenly reached critical mass. Three forces converged in the past 15 years to bring us to this moment:

- **Explosion of data**: Every click, photo, GPS signal, and online purchase generates information. Smartphones, sensors, and connected devices have created a tidal wave of data. Where early researchers struggled to find enough examples to train systems, today's models can draw on billions of samples. Data is the raw fuel that powers modern AI.

- **Immense computing power:** The rise of Graphics Processing Units (GPUs), originally built for gaming, turned out to be a game-changer. GPUs are excellent at the kind of parallel math that neural networks require. Combined with cloud computing, this made once-impossible calculations accessible to startups, researchers, and enterprises worldwide.

- **Algorithmic breakthroughs**: In 2017, researchers introduced the transformer architecture, which allowed AI systems to handle long sequences of text or data more effectively. Transformers underpin large language models like GPT, enabling coherent essays, conversations, and even software code.

Put these together, and AI leapt from the background into the spotlight. For years, it was hidden in tools like spam filters, recommendation engines, and navigation apps. But generative AI brought it directly to users: type a question, get an answer that sounds human. That shift - from silent infrastructure to visible assistant - changed perceptions almost overnight.

The adoption speed is historic. Facebook took nearly a year to reach one million users. Netflix took more than three years. ChatGPT did it in just five days. That meteoric growth made AI impossible to ignore.

Now, AI is touching almost every field at once:

- Business: customer support chatbots, predictive analytics.
- Healthcare: image analysis, drug discovery.
- Education: tutoring, personalized study guides.
- Entertainment: music generation, film editing, game design.

It's not just about capability - it's about accessibility. For the first time, anyone with an internet connection can interact directly with powerful AI. That democratization is why it feels like AI is suddenly *everywhere*.

Human Commentary

For most of my life, AI was invisible. When Spotify made a playlist for me, I didn't think of it as artificial intelligence. I just thought: "Nice, it gets my taste". That was AI, but in the background.

Then came tools like ChatGPT. Suddenly, friends who'd never cared about technology were asking, "Can it write my homework?" or "Can it plan my vacation?" That's when it clicked: AI didn't just get smarter - it got visible.

It reminds me of electricity in the early 1900s. At first, it powered factories, out of sight for most people. Then light bulbs appeared in homes, and electricity felt like magic. AI is going through the same transition. It's no longer just hidden in logistics or finance; it's sitting on your screen, answering in plain language.

The funny part is that we were already using AI daily without realizing it. The only difference now is that it talks back. And once people experience that - a tool that feels conversational, creative, and almost human - it spreads like wildfire.

That's why AI feels "sudden". It was always there. We just hadn't noticed until it started speaking our language.

Q6: What is a neural network?

AI Answer

A neural network is one of the core building blocks of modern artificial intelligence. It's a computer model inspired loosely by the human brain, designed to recognize patterns and make predictions. While the brain has billions of neurons firing electrical signals, an artificial neural network uses mathematical "nodes" connected by weighted links. Together, they can solve problems far too complex for traditional programming.

At its simplest, a neural network has three types of layers:

- **Input layer** receives raw data, like pixels from a photo or sound waves from a voice recording.
- **Hidden layers** transform the data step by step, each layer extracting more abstract features.
- **Output layer** produces the result, such as "this is a dog", "this is positive sentiment", or "translate this sentence into Spanish".

Training happens through adjustment. The network makes a guess, checks how far it is from the correct answer, and shifts its internal weights slightly. Repeat this millions of times, and the network becomes skilled at spotting patterns.

The real power of neural networks lies in their flexibility. The same architecture can be applied in very different domains:

- Weather forecasting models use them to simulate complex climate patterns and predict storms with greater accuracy.
- Earthquake monitoring systems analyze seismic vibrations to spot early tremors.
- Cybersecurity tools use them to detect unusual login behaviors or network traffic that may signal potential attacks.

This adaptability is why neural networks are at the heart of many AI breakthroughs. They don't require humans to hand-design every rule; instead, they uncover useful features automatically.

The name "neural network" can make them sound mystical, but at their core they're just layers of math - equations repeated at scale. The surprising part is what emerges when enough layers and enough data are combined: systems that can perceive, classify, and even generate information in ways that feel intelligent.

Human Commentary

The first diagram of a neural network I ever saw looked impossibly complex - circles and lines sprawled across a slide like spaghetti. I remember thinking: "I'll never understand this". Then someone compared it to passing papers down a row of students. Each student makes a tiny mark before handing it on. By the time the paper reaches the end, all those small contributions add up to a clear answer. That clicked.

What fascinates me is how the same basic setup can do wildly different things. The same kind of network that recommends me a new jazz album can also help detect seismic activity under the ocean floor. It feels almost unfair - one architecture, endless possibilities.

But it's important not to get swept up in the mystique. A neural network isn't a brain. It doesn't dream or reflect. It's math, scaled and repeated until patterns emerge. That simplicity makes its achievements even more impressive.

If I had to explain it quickly over tea, I'd say: it's a digital pattern-spotter, built in layers, that gets better the more you train it. Nothing more - but also nothing less.

Q7: How do large language models (like ChatGPT) work?

AI Answer

Large Language Models (LLMs) are a class of AI systems designed to understand and generate human-like text. At their core, they work on a surprisingly simple principle: predicting the most likely next word in a sequence. But thanks to their scale - billions of parameters and massive training datasets - the results can feel astonishingly fluent.

The breakthrough that enabled LLMs is the transformer architecture, introduced in 2017. Unlike earlier models that read text one word at a time in strict order, transformers use a mechanism called attention. Attention lets the model consider all the words in a sentence (or even a paragraph) at once, weighing how strongly each word relates to the others. That's why LLMs can maintain context across long passages instead of losing track after a few sentences.

Training an LLM involves feeding it enormous amounts of text: books, articles, websites, code repositories, and more. During training, the model guesses the next word, compares its guess to the actual word, and adjusts its internal parameters. Repeat this process trillions of times, and the model learns grammar, facts, writing styles, and reasoning patterns - though it doesn't *understand* them the way humans do.

The "parameters" are like adjustable knobs inside the model. GPT-3, for instance, has 175 billion parameters (for GPT-4 and GPT-5, OpenAI has not disclosed parameter counts, emphasizing instead improvements in reasoning, efficiency, and safety). Each knob encodes a tiny piece of information about language. When combined, they allow the system to generate essays, summarize reports, translate text, write code, or even answer questions conversationally.

Applications are broad:

- Drafting and editing business documents.
- Summarizing long reports.
- Assisting with customer service.
- Generating computer code.
- Brainstorming creative ideas.

But LLMs also have limitations. They can produce "hallucinations" - answers that sound plausible but are factually wrong. They may also reflect biases in their training data. This is why human oversight is crucial: models are powerful, but not infallible.

What makes LLMs remarkable is their accessibility. For the first time, advanced AI isn't confined to research labs or tech giants. Anyone can type a prompt and watch a machine generate language that feels natural and, at times, surprisingly insightful.

Human Commentary

The first time I tried ChatGPT, I asked it to draft a polite reminder email to a client who was late on payment. Ten seconds later, I had a polished draft ready to send. I remember staring at the screen thinking, "Okay, this is different".

Since then, I've used language models for everything from analyzing markets to brainstorming blog posts. Sometimes they give me insights I wouldn't have thought of; sometimes they generate nonsense. Either way, the speed is unmatched.

What strikes me most is how human the interaction feels. You type in plain English, and it replies in plain English. No menus, no coding, no technical jargon. That's why people who never cared about AI suddenly find it useful - the barrier to entry is gone.

Still, it's easy to forget that behind the friendly tone, there's no actual understanding. I like to describe ChatGPT as a predictive text system on steroids. It doesn't know what it's saying, but it's incredibly good at stringing words together in ways that feel natural. The trick is remembering that it's a partner for drafting and brainstorming, not a source of truth.

Used wisely, it's like having an endlessly patient co-writer - one who never runs out of words.

Q8: How much data does AI need to learn?

AI Answer

The amount of data AI needs depends on the complexity of the task. For simple problems, a few thousand examples can be enough. For highly complex tasks - like generating realistic text, images, or speech - the requirements grow into billions of examples.

Take handwritten digit recognition as an illustration. The famous MNIST dataset, with 70,000 examples of digits 0–9, is sufficient for models to achieve near-perfect accuracy. But training a large language model like GPT requires terabytes of text from books, websites, and articles. Writing natural, human-like language isn't just about grammar; it requires exposure to style, context, and world knowledge - and that demands far more data.

Why so much? Because AI learns by spotting patterns. Simple tasks have limited patterns, while complex ones involve subtle relationships. To capture those, models need more examples.

But "more" isn't always better. Quality matters as much as quantity. A model trained on biased, repetitive, or error-filled data will learn those flaws. For example, a medical AI trained only on one demographic group may struggle to diagnose patients from another. Likewise, a chatbot trained mostly in English will perform poorly in underrepresented languages.

Researchers are working on ways to reduce data requirements. Transfer learning allows a model trained on one task to adapt to another with less data. Few-shot learning lets models pick up new skills from only a handful of examples. These techniques mean that smaller organizations, not just tech giants, can build useful models.

Still, the "data hunger" of AI remains a challenge. Training the most advanced systems requires not just vast datasets but also enormous computing resources. That's why frontier models are typically developed by companies with both the data and the hardware to support them.

The bottom line: AI doesn't just need a lot of data - it needs the right kind of data. Clean, diverse, and representative information produces systems that are reliable and fair. In other words: the quality of the input always determines the quality of the output.

Human Commentary

I like to compare AI training to cooking. Give a chef a hundred high-quality recipes, and they can prepare almost anything well. Give them a million sloppy ones, and the results will be confusing at best. AI is the same: the quality of its "ingredients" matters more than sheer volume.

I've seen this firsthand when experimenting with prompts. If I ask a vague question, the AI produces a vague answer. But when I provide clear, detailed instructions, the output suddenly becomes sharper and more useful. It's not that the model has changed - it's the *data I gave it*. The input shapes the output.

Another reality is that AI doesn't work without a human teacher. Even this book didn't just "write itself". Sure, I leaned on AI to draft ideas, but it still took hours of organizing, rephrasing, and clarifying. I had to guide it, much like a teacher guiding a student through an assignment.

That's why I think of AI less as a genius and more as a very eager apprentice. It can absorb information at a scale we can't imagine, but it needs direction, structure, and quality material. Without that, it just serves up noise.

Q9: Does AI understand, or just predict?

AI Answer

This is one of the most philosophical questions about AI. Does it "understand" anything, or is it just sophisticated prediction?

Most experts agree: AI predicts. Large language models like ChatGPT don't truly grasp meaning; they calculate probabilities. Given the words "the sky is", they predict "blue" is more likely than "banana". Over billions of examples, the predictions become astonishingly accurate, giving the illusion of understanding.

Humans, however, process meaning. We don't just predict the next word - we connect language to experience. If I say, "It's raining cats and dogs", you know it's not literal because you've seen storms and you understand metaphors. AI can mimic this by exposure to millions of idioms, but it doesn't *experience* rain.

This is why AI sometimes "hallucinates". It generates plausible-sounding but false statements. It's predicting patterns without grounding in reality. True understanding would require not just patterns, but consciousness and lived experience.

Still, predictions can be powerful. In translation, prediction works well enough to create useful tools. In medicine, prediction can flag anomalies. So, while AI may not "understand", its predictive power can still have enormous value.

Human Commentary

I've seen colleagues treat AI almost like a consultant, saying, "Let's see what it thinks about this strategy". But AI doesn't think - it calculates. It doesn't form opinions, it doesn't believe, it doesn't care. It predicts what words are most likely to follow others.

I once asked an AI for a business plan. The answer looked impressive at first glance: clear structure, professional tone, lots of buzzwords. But when I read carefully, it was generic, like a template with no understanding of my market or clients. It was prediction dressed up as insight.

The way I explain it to friends is this: AI is like a library index that can generate sentences. It knows where words and ideas tend to appear together, but it has never read the book cover to cover. You, on the other hand, know what those words *mean*.

That doesn't make AI useless - far from it. Its predictions are incredibly powerful tools. But the key is remembering the line: AI predicts patterns, humans understand meaning. When you combine the two, you get something far stronger than either alone.

Q10: Is AI creative?

AI Answer

Creativity is often described as one of the most uniquely human traits - the ability to generate ideas, art, or solutions that feel original and meaningful. But can machines be creative? The answer depends on how we define creativity.

AI systems today can compose music, paint pictures, write poems, design logos, and even propose scientific hypotheses. They do this by training on vast datasets - for example, thousands of songs or artworks - and learning the patterns of style, structure, and composition. Once trained, they can combine and remix those patterns in new ways. That's why tools like DALL·E or ChatGPT can generate outputs that surprise us: they fuse patterns into combinations we might never have considered.

Some argue that this *is* creativity. After all, much of human creativity also builds on existing ideas. Shakespeare borrowed plots, Picasso absorbed traditions, and jazz musicians riff on scales. By this logic, AI recombination counts as creative expression. If it produces something new and valuable, why not call it creativity?

Others argue AI creativity is an illusion. While AI produces novel outputs, it doesn't have intention, emotion, or purpose. A human artist paints to express joy, grief, or curiosity. An AI generates because it was told to. It doesn't know what sadness feels like, or why beauty moves us. The difference lies in motivation: humans create for meaning, AI generates from probability.

Still, AI creativity is already reshaping industries. Designers use AI for rapid brainstorming. Musicians co-create melodies with algorithms. Writers rely on AI for drafting, editing, or sparking ideas. In science, AI proposes molecular structures or equations that lead to new research directions. Sometimes the "machine imagination" feels almost alien - offering solutions humans might never see.

The risks are real too. Copyright disputes are unfolding as artists argue that training on their work without permission amounts to theft. AI-generated content could flood markets, making authentic human art harder to recognize or undervalued. And overreliance on AI tools might dull human skills if we outsource too much of the creative process.

In short, AI can generate novelty, and in practice it can feel creative. But whether that's "true creativity" depends on your definition. If creativity is simply producing something new, then yes, AI qualifies. If it requires intention and lived experience, then no - it remains uniquely human. What's clear is that AI has expanded what creativity looks like, making it faster, more collaborative, and more accessible than ever.

Human Commentary

The first time I asked an AI to write a story, I caught myself smiling at the result - it wasn't perfect, but it was clever, even funny. For a moment, I forgot it was "just a program". That, to me, captures both the wonder and the tension: it *feels* creative, but I know there's no spark behind it.

What fascinates me is how useful it is as a partner. When I'm stuck, AI can throw out ideas I wouldn't have thought of. It's like brainstorming with someone who has read every book, seen every painting, and listened to every song. Sometimes it inspires me, sometimes it misses the mark - but it always pushes me further.

Still, I don't confuse it with human creativity. When a friend writes a song, I value it not just for the melody, but for the story behind it - their breakup, their joy, their memories. That's something AI can't replicate. Its outputs may move me, but the *meaning* comes from me, not from it.

So is AI creative? Functionally, yes. Philosophically, maybe not. But either way, it changes the landscape. It democratizes creation, it challenges us to rethink originality, and it forces us to ask what we value most: the product, or the human story behind it.

Chapter 2: Inside the Machine

With the basics covered, it's time to peek under the hood. This chapter takes us inside the machine itself, showing how algorithms, learning, and neural networks really work.

Q11: What are algorithms, and why are they important in AI?

AI Answer

An algorithm is essentially a process, a structured way of solving a problem. Imagine you're asked to sort a deck of cards. One person might go through the deck and arrange it by number, another might separate by suit first. Both approaches are algorithms: different paths to the same goal.

In AI, algorithms are more than recipes. They are problem-solving strategies. Take route planning: when you ask a navigation app for the fastest way to work, it doesn't just check one road. It evaluates multiple possibilities simultaneously, weighing distance, real-time traffic, and even historical data. The algorithm is the logic that makes such rapid comparisons possible.

Different algorithms serve different purposes. A decision tree asks a series of yes/no questions. A random forest combines many such trees and takes a majority vote, often improving accuracy. Gradient descent is one of the most important algorithms in AI: it powers the training of neural networks by gradually adjusting their internal "weights" until predictions improve.

The choice of algorithm often determines whether an AI system succeeds. A hospital might prefer an algorithm that highlights patterns in medical scans, even if it's complex. A bank detecting fraud might favor something simpler and more interpretable, so humans can understand the logic behind each decision.

But algorithms also reveal one of AI's weaknesses: they don't have values or morals. They follow the instructions and the data they're given. If the data is biased, the algorithm faithfully reproduces that bias. This is why evaluation and oversight are critical - not to fix the math, but to check the goals and assumptions behind it.

In short: algorithms are the engines under the hood of AI. You may not see them directly, but they determine how powerful, reliable, and trustworthy the system really is.

Human Commentary

I often hear people talk about "the algorithm" like it's a mysterious force running our lives. "The algorithm hid my post". "The algorithm showed me this video". It almost sounds like an invisible boss. But really, it's just a set of rules, optimized for goals we set.

That doesn't mean it's harmless. I've noticed how algorithms shape my daily routines in subtle ways. A playlist app once kept feeding me songs from the same style until I felt stuck in a musical loop. The algorithm wasn't trying to trap me - it was simply optimizing for what it thought I liked. Still, the effect was real: less variety, less discovery.

What really struck me is how different algorithms fit different needs. In sales, I wanted tools that were transparent so I could explain results to clients. In social media, the priority is usually engagement, not clarity. The algorithm itself isn't "good" or "bad" - it's the objective we give it that makes the difference.

So, every time someone says "The algorithm decided", I remind myself: "No, humans decided the goals. The algorithm just did its job".

Q12: What is machine learning, really?

AI Answer

Machine learning (ML) is a branch of artificial intelligence where computers learn patterns from data and improve their performance over time without being explicitly programmed with every rule.

In traditional programming, humans had to spell out all the rules. If you wanted to recommend products in the 1990s, you might program: "If customer buys shoes, also suggest socks". But shoppers change habits quickly, and static rules break down.

Machine learning flips this logic. Instead of writing every rule, we feed the computer thousands of examples of browsing and purchase histories. The system then figures out the patterns for itself - maybe seasonal demand shifts, complementary products often bought together, or unusual return patterns. It doesn't 'understand' shopping the way we do, but it recognizes statistical cues that separate typical behavior from unusual ones.

At the heart of ML is the training loop:

1. The model makes a prediction.
2. It checks the prediction against the correct answer.
3. It adjusts its internal settings slightly.
4. Repeat this millions of times until it gets consistently better.

The real strength of ML is its adaptability. Unlike a hard-coded program, an ML model keeps learning as new data arrives. That's why banks use it to detect evolving fraud patterns and e-commerce sites rely on it to recommend products as tastes shift.

But adaptability also means vulnerability. If the data is biased, the system will learn the bias. A hiring model trained mostly on male résumés might unfairly disadvantage female candidates. A medical model trained only on one population might misdiagnose others. Machine learning doesn't question its lessons - it absorbs whatever data we give it.

In Chapter 1, we saw that ML can take different forms depending on how the data is presented. In the next two questions, we'll look more closely at these learning styles: first supervised vs. unsupervised learning, then reinforcement learning. For now, remember: machine learning is not one technique, but a family of methods that allow computers to detect patterns, adapt, and improve - making them flexible in a way traditional programs never were.

Human Commentary

When I first tried to explain machine learning to a friend, I said: "It's when computers teach themselves". That sounded impressive, but also misleading. They don't really "teach themselves" - they repeat, adjust, and repeat again until the pattern clicks. It's less like a genius in the making, and more like a very stubborn student who never stops practicing.

What I find most striking is how much of it happens invisibly. I don't think about ML when an online store recommends the next item I might need, or when a streaming service quietly adjusts my suggestions based on what I've been watching. Even the grammar checker nudging me right now is running on ML. These systems shape my digital life without announcing themselves.

And yet, the invisibility makes it easy to overestimate them. I once watched my phone autocorrect "ciao" into "chaos". Amusing, but also a reminder: ML doesn't understand meaning. It just knows patterns.

So when people ask me what machine learning really is, I say: *"it's computers getting good at spotting patterns in data - sometimes so good it feels like intelligence"*. But it's still pattern-spotting, not understanding.

Q13: What's the difference between supervised and unsupervised learning?

AI Answer

In Chapter 1, we introduced the main ways AI can learn. Now let's zoom into two of the most widely used: supervised and unsupervised learning.

Supervised learning is like learning with an answer key. The system is trained on examples where both the input and the correct output are known. For instance, if you want a model to recognize handwritten numbers, you give it thousands of images labeled "0", "1", "2", and so on. The system adjusts itself until it can reliably match new, unseen images to the correct labels.

Supervised learning is especially good for prediction tasks: given new data, what's the right category, number, or label? It powers applications such as:

- Predicting house prices from neighborhood data.
- Predicting whether a loan applicant will repay.
- Forecasting crop yields from satellite images.

Unsupervised learning, by contrast, doesn't come with labeled answers. The system only gets the raw inputs and must find patterns by itself. Think of feeding it thousands of shopping transactions. Without knowing who bought what, the system might group customers into segments - frequent bargain hunters, luxury shoppers, or seasonal buyers. Nobody told it those groups existed; it discovered them from the data.

Unsupervised learning is useful for discovery tasks, like:

- Customer segmentation in marketing.
- Detecting unusual activity in network traffic.
- Compressing data by finding efficient representations.

There are also hybrid methods. Semi-supervised learning combines a small set of labeled data with a large pool of unlabeled data, helpful in fields like medicine where labels are costly. And self-supervised learning - a newer technique - creates its own training signals by predicting missing parts of data (for example, predicting the next word in a sentence). Many modern language models use this method.

The key distinction: supervised learning is about mapping inputs to known outputs, while unsupervised learning is about uncovering hidden structures when no labels exist.

Human Commentary

When I try to explain this to friends, I use teaching styles as an analogy. Supervised learning is like school exams: you have practice questions and the correct answers, so you learn by checking your mistakes against the key. Unsupervised learning is like wandering in a library with no guidance, slowly grouping books by theme as you notice connections.

I've seen both in action. "Supervised learning" shows up in my online banking app - the reason suspicious transactions get flagged instantly. Unsupervised learning pops up in my photo app, which magically creates a "beach vacations" album without me tagging a single picture. Two very different paths, but both surprisingly useful.

Personally, unsupervised learning reminds me of my early sales career. Nobody gave me neat categories for clients. I just started spotting patterns: this group loved detailed data, that group preferred quick calls. Over time, I clustered them - not because someone told me to, but because the signals were there.

That's the essence: sometimes we learn with a teacher, sometimes by exploring on our own. AI, like us, needs both approaches.

Q14: What is reinforcement learning?

AI Answer

Alongside supervised and unsupervised methods, there's a third major approach: reinforcement learning (RL). Instead of learning from fixed examples, RL is about learning through experience - trial and error guided by rewards.

Think of training a dog. Perform a trick correctly, get a treat. Do nothing or misbehave, get no reward. Over time, the dog learns which actions maximize rewards. Reinforcement learning works the same way, except the "dog" is an algorithm, and the "treats" are mathematical reward signals.

An RL system has three parts:

1. **Agent:** the learner or decision-maker (the AI).
2. **Environment**: the world it interacts with (a game, a robot's surroundings, a financial market).
3. **Reward signal:** feedback about performance (points scored, profit earned, fewer collisions).

The cycle works like this: the agent takes an action, the environment responds, and the agent updates its strategy (called a policy). Over thousands or millions of iterations, the agent learns behaviors that maximize long-term rewards.

This approach has fueled some of AI's most famous breakthroughs. AlphaGo, the program that beat world champions at the game Go, used reinforcement learning to master strategies humans had never imagined. Robotics use RL to teach machines to walk, grasp, or balance. Self-driving cars apply RL principles to make rapid decisions about speed and steering in unpredictable traffic.

RL is powerful because it allows AI to discover strategies humans might miss. Sometimes, agents even find loopholes in the rules, exploiting them in surprising ways. But it also has challenges:

- It often requires enormous amounts of training data.
- It can be unstable, with agents learning bizarre behaviors if the reward isn't defined carefully.
- It demands significant computing power, making it resource intensive.

Despite these hurdles, reinforcement learning remains one of the most exciting frontiers of AI - because it mirrors how living beings learn from interaction, not just instruction.

Human Commentary

When I first learned about reinforcement learning, it reminded me of how I improved in sales. Nobody handed me a perfect script. I tried things, got reactions, and adjusted. A positive client response felt like a "reward". An awkward silence felt like a "penalty". Over time, I built a strategy that worked.

What fascinates me most is how RL sometimes finds solutions that humans never think of. In one case I read about, an RL agent trained to play a video game found a way to rack up points by exploiting a glitch the designers hadn't considered. It wasn't "cheating" - it was simply maximizing the reward in the system it was given.

That made me smile, because it shows RL isn't just about copying human strategies. Sometimes it stumbles on completely new ones. And that's both exciting and a little unsettling.

The takeaway for me is simple: reinforcement learning teaches us that intelligence - human or machine - often doesn't come from rules but from experience. We don't always need a teacher. Sometimes we just need to try, fail, and learn.

Q15: Why is deep learning considered a breakthrough compared to other types of machine learning?

AI Answer

Earlier, we saw how deep learning fits within the broader picture of AI and machine learning. Here, let's explore why it has been such a game-changer.

Deep learning is a specialized branch of machine learning that relies on multi-layered neural networks. The word "deep" refers to the many stacked layers between input and output, which let the system build increasingly abstract representations.

Traditional ML approaches often required humans to define useful features. For example, in fraud detection, an analyst might feed in variables like "transaction size" or "location mismatch". The model could only learn from what it was given. Deep learning revolutionized this process: instead of relying on handcrafted signals, networks automatically discover what matters during training. In an image system, lower layers might highlight edges, middle layers combine them into shapes, and deeper layers recognize entire objects.

This shift enabled breakthroughs across industries. In vision, self-driving cars can identify pedestrians and road signs. In language, systems translate text, correct grammar, and power generative AI models. In science, DL predicts protein structures or simulates climate processes. Its strength lies not only in accuracy but also in scale: modern networks can have billions of parameters, trained on massive datasets with GPUs or TPUs.

But power comes with challenges. Deep networks act like "black boxes" - they produce results but are hard to interpret. They also require enormous data and energy, raising concerns in fields like medicine, finance, and sustainability. Bias in training data can amplify unfair outcomes.

In short: all deep learning is machine learning, but not all machine learning is deep learning. DL is considered a breakthrough because it automated feature discovery, scaled to unprecedented complexity, and opened new frontiers once thought unreachable - from driverless cars to cutting-edge scientific discovery.

Human Commentary

When I first heard "deep learning", I imagined something mystical - like plunging into hidden waters of intelligence. In reality, it's more like stacking floors in a skyscraper. The ground floor processes simple things; the higher you go, the more complete the view becomes. By the top, the system sees the whole city. That's what deep learning does: each layer adds perspective until the full picture emerges.

What fascinates me is how this layering principle unlocked so many technologies we now take for granted. Without it, my phone wouldn't recognize my face, my voice assistant wouldn't understand me, and I certainly wouldn't be writing this book with the help of ChatGPT.

Yet, deep learning feels both impressive and fragile. I've read about cases where a network could detect financial fraud patterns invisible to humans - and then failed spectacularly if a transaction record is slightly altered. That mix of brilliance and brittleness makes me see it less as a perfect system and more as an extraordinary but quirky tool.

For me, the key is remembering that deep learning isn't about depth of wisdom. It's about depth of layers - and how those layers, when stacked right, can build astonishing results.

Q16: How do neural networks work?

AI Answer

To understand why neural networks became the foundation of modern AI, we need to go one step deeper: how they actually work.

A neural network is a system of interconnected nodes arranged in layers. Each connection carries a weight, which represents how strongly one node influences another. Data enters at the input layer, flows through hidden layers of calculations, and produces an output.

The crucial mechanism is backpropagation. When the network gets something wrong - say it labels a cat as a dog - an error signal flows backward through the layers. Each weight is nudged slightly to reduce the error. Repeating this process millions of times gradually tunes the network to perform accurately on new, unseen data. This ability to self-correct is what turned neural networks from a curiosity into a revolution.

Different network types specialize in different problems:

- Convolutional Neural Networks (CNNs) detect visual features like edges, shapes, and textures, which is why they dominate image recognition.
- Recurrent Neural Networks (RNNs) and their successor, Transformers, process sequences, making them ideal for language, music, and time-series data.
- GANs (Generative Adversarial Networks) pit two networks against each other - one generates data, the other critiques - producing realistic images, audio, or video.

Yet, neural networks come with trade-offs. Their complexity makes them powerful but opaque. Unlike a simple decision tree where you can trace the logic, a deep network may involve billions of parameters, making it hard to explain why it gave a certain answer. This "black box" problem is a major issue in medicine, law, and finance.

Another challenge is cost. Training large networks demands massive computing power and energy. For frontier models, training runs can cost millions of dollars and consume enough electricity to power small towns. There's growing concern about the environmental footprint of these systems.

Finally, there's fragility. Neural networks can achieve superhuman accuracy on benchmark tests, yet fail in odd ways. Change a few pixels in a photo, and an image-recognition system might mistake a panda for a gibbon. Their strength - sensitivity to patterns - can also make them vulnerable.

Despite these issues, neural networks remain the workhorses of AI. Their layered design makes them astonishingly versatile, and their ability to learn representations automatically keeps pushing the field forward. They are not brains, but they're close enough to raise profound questions about the nature of intelligence.

Human Commentary

When I finally learned about backpropagation, it felt like discovering the trick behind a magic show. Suddenly the mystery of "how does it learn?" became clear: trial, error, correction - just at an unimaginable scale. It made the whole concept feel less like science fiction and more like engineering.

What impresses me most is how fragile and powerful these systems are at the same time. I've read about networks that detect cancer earlier than doctors, and others that get fooled by a sticker on a stop sign. That contradiction captures both the promise and the risk.

For me, the lesson is humility. Neural networks aren't "thinking" machines - they're mathematical mirrors of the data we feed them. When trained well, they seem brilliant. When trained poorly, they reveal just how brittle they are.

If I had to summarize: neural networks work by layering simple math until complexity emerges. They're less like brains and more like engines - intricate, costly, and immensely powerful when tuned correctly.

Q17: Why do people say data is the "fuel" of AI?

AI Answer

The saying "data is the fuel of AI" comes from the fact that without data, AI simply cannot function. Just as a car engine can't run without fuel, an AI model cannot learn or make predictions without data.

Think of smart home speaker. To tell the difference between a command and background noise, it must be trained on thousands - ideally millions - of audio samples. From those examples, it learns patterns: speech rhythms, tone, and signal frequencies. Without that training data, the assistant would have no basis for judgment.

The analogy goes further. Just as low-grade materials weaken a building, poor-quality data weakens AI. If a dataset is mislabeled or outdated, the model's predictions will suffer. And if the data reflects bias, the AI will reproduce that bias. Facial recognition systems, for instance, have been shown to perform poorly on underrepresented groups when their training data lacked diversity.

Different AI tasks require very different amounts of data. Predicting house prices might work with a few thousand examples. Training a large language model like GPT, on the other hand, requires trillions of words from books, websites, and articles. The complexity of the task determines the hunger for data.

Unlike fuel in a car, however, data isn't consumed in the same way. It can be reused, combined, and repurposed. But this creates new challenges: who owns the data, who controls it, and who benefits from it? Companies collect enormous amounts of personal information - browsing history, GPS trails, purchase records - often without users realizing how valuable it is. Privacy and fairness remain central debates.

Researchers are also working on ways to reduce data dependence. Synthetic data (artificially generated examples), transfer learning (reusing models trained on one task for another), and few-shot learning (teaching models from just a handful of examples) are all helping. But for now, most cutting-edge AI remains data-hungry.

So, when people call data the "fuel of AI", they're right. It powers training, testing, and improvement. But unlike gasoline, it isn't scarce - it's everywhere. The real challenge is making sure it's accurate, diverse, and used responsibly.

Human Commentary

When I hear "data is the new oil", I think about how much of my daily life generates little drops of that fuel. Every time I tap my card, scroll through a feed, or use GPS, I'm adding to someone's dataset. It's fascinating - and a little unsettling.

In my work, I've seen firsthand how data quality makes or breaks a project. Give AI sloppy, incomplete information, and it produces nonsense. Feed it clean, structured data, and it can uncover insights that surprise even the experts. It reminds me of writing this book: when I asked vague questions, I got vague answers. When I refined the questions, the answers suddenly became sharper.

The unsettling part is how invisible the process feels. My playlists, my news feed, even my grocery app are shaped by data I didn't consciously choose to share. I'm not against it - often it makes life easier. But it does make me think about ownership. Whose fuel is it really?

For me, the lesson is simple: AI doesn't think, it eats data. And just like any engine, the quality of what you put in determines how far and how smoothly it can go.

Q18: What is natural language processing (NLP)?

AI Answer

Natural Language Processing (NLP) is the branch of AI that focuses on enabling computers to understand, interpret, and generate human language. Language is one of the most complex aspects of intelligence: it's full of ambiguity, slang, metaphor, and cultural nuance. NLP is the bridge that allows machines to work with words.

At its simplest, NLP is about turning language into numbers. Computers don't "understand" text directly - they represent words as mathematical vectors. In these vector spaces, words that are similar in meaning are close together. For instance, "king" and "queen" might be near each other, while "banana" is far away. These representations allow models to analyze and manipulate text mathematically.

NLP covers a wide range of tasks:

- Classification: detecting sentiment in product reviews, identifying toxic comments in forums.
- Translation: services like Google Translate or DeepL.
- Search: retrieving the most relevant documents.
- Summarization: condensing long articles.
- Question answering: powering systems like ChatGPT.

Earlier NLP systems relied on rules: manually coded grammar structures, syntax trees, and dictionaries. They worked in narrow contexts but struggled with the messiness of real language.

The breakthrough came with statistical methods, and later with deep learning. Word embeddings like Word2Vec (2013) captured meaning in numerical form. Then transformers (2017) made it possible to process long passages and capture context more effectively. This leap gave rise to today's large language models, which are essentially advanced NLP systems scaled up massively.

NLP is now embedded in everyday life: voice assistants transcribe speech, grammar checkers polish writing, search engines parse our queries, and customer service bots provide answers.

Yet challenges remain. Sarcasm, humor, and cultural context often trip up AI. A phrase like "Yeah, right" can mean agreement or skepticism depending on tone. Humans rely on shared experience to interpret such subtleties; NLP models only have patterns in data.

So, while NLP has become remarkably capable, it's still about pattern recognition, not true comprehension.

Human Commentary

I always find NLP a little magical. The fact that I can type a question in plain English and get a useful response from a machine still feels futuristic, even though I now use it daily.

What impresses me is how much it has improved. I remember early translation tools that made Italian sound robotic and clumsy in English.

Today, I can paste whole paragraphs into a translator and get results good enough for business. Not flawless, but practical.

Working on this book has made me realize how much NLP quietly surrounds me. A grammar checker suggests better phrasing. My phone predicts the next word in a text. Even the search bar in a shopping app is powered by it. None of it calls attention to itself, but it's there - shaping how I read and write every day.

Still, NLP isn't perfect. I once joked with a chatbot and got a painfully literal response. It didn't "get" the humor. That's when I remind myself: it's not truly understanding, just mapping patterns.

And yet, even with those limits, NLP feels like one of the most transformative bridges between humans and machines.

Q19: How do AI systems "see" images or videos?

AI Answer

When we talk about AI "seeing", what we really mean is converting visual data into numbers that algorithms can analyze. A digital image is nothing more than a grid of pixels, each pixel holding a value for color and brightness. To a computer, a photo of a cat isn't a furry creature - it's a giant table of numbers.

The challenge is turning those numbers into meaningful patterns. That's where computer vision comes in.

A common approach uses convolutional neural networks (CNNs). Instead of analyzing the entire image at once, CNNs look at small regions - like scanning with a magnifying glass. Early layers detect simple features such as edges or corners. Deeper layers combine these into more complex shapes like eyes or whiskers. By the final layers, the system can identify entire objects - "this cluster of pixels is a cat".

Videos add another layer of complexity. AI must process not only individual frames but also how they change over time. Specialized architectures, often combining CNNs with recurrent networks or transformers, allow systems to recognize actions (a person waving) or track movement across frames.

Applications are everywhere:

- Facial recognition for unlocking phones or verifying identity.
- Autonomous vehicles detecting pedestrians, signs, and traffic lights.
- Wildlife Conservation: using drones to track endangered species.
- Retail tracking inventory through cameras.
- Content moderation scanning billions of uploaded images and videos.

Like other AI fields, computer vision faces challenges. Systems can be fooled by adversarial examples - tiny pixel changes invisible to humans but enough to mislead the AI. Bias in training data can also cause uneven performance, especially in facial recognition across different demographics.

Despite these hurdles, computer vision has transformed industries. A task that once demanded human experts, such as analyzing thousands of satellite images for climate research, can now be scaled up with AI support - sometimes matching or even surpassing human accuracy.

In essence, AI doesn't "see" like we do. It doesn't perceive color or depth emotionally. But through layers of math, it can turn raw pixels into useful insights - giving machines a kind of artificial sight.

Human Commentary

The first time my phone created an automatic "memories" video from my photos, I laughed. It grouped my friends, added music, and stitched moments together. I knew it wasn't really "seeing", but it felt oddly personal - as if the phone had peeked into my life and told me a story back.

What fascinates me most is how computer vision sometimes catches things we don't. In healthcare, AI has spotted early signs of disease that even trained doctors missed. On the flip side, I've also seen funny mistakes, like an AI labeling a photo of a blueberry muffin as a chihuahua. Both moments remind me: it's brilliant, but not infallible.

In daily life, I barely notice it anymore. Unlocking my phone with my face, boarding a plane by scanning a QR code, tagging friends in photos - it all feels casual. Yet, if I stop and think, it's profound: machines that once only calculated now "observe".

For me, that's the essence of computer vision: it doesn't see beauty or meaning, but it gives us tools that extend our own eyes. And sometimes, those tools show us what we might have missed.

Q20: What is the difference between narrow AI and general AI?

AI Answer

Understanding the difference between narrow AI and general AI helps clarify where we are today versus where we might be headed.

Narrow AI (also called weak AI) refers to systems built for specific tasks. A chess engine, a spam filter, a facial recognition app, or a voice assistant - each is optimized for one domain. Some narrow AIs outperform humans in their niche, but they can't transfer their skills elsewhere. A system that diagnoses X-rays can't also translate Italian poetry.

General AI (AGI) is the hypothetical goal of creating machines with broad, human-like intelligence. An AGI would not only excel in one domain but also adapt across many - reasoning, learning, and applying knowledge flexibly. It could play chess, cook dinner, and write a poem, all without needing to be retrained from scratch.

Today's AI, even the most advanced, is still narrow. ChatGPT, for instance, can generate essays but doesn't know how to drive a car. A self-driving system can navigate roads but can't explain a joke. Humans, by contrast, naturally transfer skills: learning to ride a bicycle makes it easier to pick up a motorcycle.

The prospect of AGI excites some and alarms others. Optimists imagine breakthroughs in science, medicine, and productivity. Skeptics point to risks: loss of human control, misaligned goals, and ethical dilemmas if AGI surpasses us. Predictions vary wildly - some researchers think AGI could emerge this century, others doubt it will ever be possible.

For businesses and policymakers, the distinction matters. Narrow AI is what we have today: powerful but specialized. AGI remains speculative. Confusing the two leads to misplaced expectations - or misplaced fears.

In short: narrow AI solves specific problems, general AI would think across problems. The first is real and all around us; the second is still an open question.

Human Commentary

I often smile when people talk about AI as if it's already a digital brain. A friend once told me, after trying ChatGPT: "It knows everything!" I didn't want to ruin the moment, but I thought: sure, it knows a lot of text - but ask it to fix a leaky faucet and you'll see the limit.

For me, narrow AI feels like meeting a brilliant specialist. I once worked with a colleague who could negotiate contracts like a master but couldn't manage a simple spreadsheet. General AI, if it ever exists, would be like that rare person who can do a bit of everything: play music, fix the printer, lead a meeting, and still crack a joke at dinner.

We're not there - not even close. And maybe that's a good thing for now. Part of what makes us human is exactly that mix of skills, emotions, and improvisation.

So, when I hear talk about AGI, I take it with both curiosity and caution. For now, the AI around me isn't general. It's narrow - but powerful enough that it's already reshaping how I work and live.

Chapter 3: AI in Action

Now that we've looked inside the machine, it's time to see where AI is already changing the world around us - industry by industry. From hospitals to farms, factories to space, AI is moving from theory to action.

Q21: How is AI used in healthcare?

AI Answer

Healthcare is one of the most promising areas for AI because it combines two ingredients the technology thrives on: data and high-stakes decisions. From patient care to research, AI is already making a difference.

One major use is in diagnostics. Instead of relying only on what a human doctor can see, AI systems can analyze medical records to predict which patients are at risk of hospital readmission, helping hospitals intervene earlier and reduce strain on staff. AI is also making progress through AI-powered home monitoring systems that track sleep patterns, nutrition, or medication adherence, sending early alerts to both patients and doctors before a crisis develops. These tools act as a second set of eyes and ears rather than a replacement, giving clinicians more time to focus on complex decisions.

Drug discovery is another frontier. Traditional methods of testing molecules can take years. AI accelerates this by predicting which compounds are most likely to succeed, dramatically shortening timelines and lowering costs. This approach is now being used to suggest new antibiotic candidates, design personalized cancer treatments, and even model how viruses might evolve - areas where traditional labs often struggle with speed.

AI also supports personalized medicine. By analyzing genetic information, lifestyle data, and medical history, systems can suggest tailored treatment plans instead of one-size-fits-all approaches. Hospitals are also using AI for operational tasks: scheduling, bed allocation, and predicting which departments will see surges in demand.

Of course, the stakes are high. A wrong prediction in healthcare can cost lives, not just inconvenience. That's why most experts emphasize AI as an assistive tool rather than a replacement for clinicians. The best results come from human–AI collaboration: the speed and scale of machines combined with the judgment and empathy of doctors.

Human Commentary

Healthcare is the area where I feel the promise of AI most strongly, but also where I feel the weight of caution. It's one thing if AI suggests me the wrong song; it's another if it mislabels a scan. That said, I can't ignore how impressive it already is.

What I notice around me is how many people now go to ChatGPT or other AI tools before they go to a doctor. They type in their symptoms, ask for possible causes, and sometimes even for advice on what tests they should consider. Of course, AI can't replace a professional consultation, but it shows how much people already trust it as a first step - a sort of modern "Dr. Google", only more conversational.

For me, the key is balance. I wouldn't want AI to be the final authority on my health, but I can see how it helps people feel informed and prepared before talking to a doctor. In fact, I've noticed that when I walk into a consultation knowing more, the conversation with the doctor is often sharper, more focused. AI, in that sense, can empower patients to become active participants in their own care - as long as we never forget who has the real expertise.

Q22: How is AI used in finance?

AI Answer

Finance has been one of the earliest adopters of AI, and for a good reason: financial markets generate vast amounts of data, and small improvements in analysis can mean enormous profits. AI is now deeply embedded in everything, from consumer banking to high-frequency trading.

One of the most visible uses is fraud detection. Banks process millions of transactions daily, and AI systems now flag irregular transfers within seconds - sometimes even freezing suspicious payments before they're completed.

Insurance companies are also turning to AI, using it to detect fraudulent claims by spotting inconsistencies across thousands of documents. These systems use machine learning to continuously adapt to new strategies, catching risks that would slip past older rule-based systems.

Credit scoring is another area transformed by AI. Traditional credit scores rely on relatively limited data: income, repayment history, outstanding loans. AI models can incorporate far more information, from utility payments to transaction patterns, to assess creditworthiness more accurately. This expands financial access to people who may not fit traditional criteria.

In trading and investment, AI powers algorithmic trading systems that analyze market signals and execute trades in microseconds. Hedge funds use predictive models to anticipate price movements, while robo-advisors like Betterment or Wealthfront use AI to create personalized portfolios for everyday investors.

AI is also used in customer service. Chatbots handle routine banking queries, while AI-driven systems help call center staff provide faster responses. Document processing, such as loan applications or compliance checks, is increasingly automated.

Risk management is another critical use. AI models assess exposure to currency fluctuations, credit defaults, or market downturns. During volatile times, these systems can provide more responsive insights than traditional models.

But the use of AI in finance raises concerns. Algorithmic trading, for example, has been linked to "flash crashes" where automated systems trigger sudden market swings. Bias in AI-driven credit scoring can also perpetuate inequalities if not carefully monitored. And, of course, privacy and security remain paramount when handling sensitive financial data.

Human Commentary

I don't work in finance, but I do work with numbers on the business side, so I can easily see why AI has become such a natural fit in this field. Numbers are full of patterns, and AI is built to find and use patterns faster than any human could.

On the personal side, I've also started using AI for investment suggestions. Not to replace my own decisions, but to explore different perspectives - like asking it to calculate portfolio diversification or to test different allocation scenarios. It feels a bit like having a personal advisor - unpaid, available 24/7, and endlessly patient. Of course, I still need to apply my own judgment, but it adds an interesting layer to how I approach investments.

That balance is important to me: AI as a tool for insights, not as the final decision-maker. After all, money is something I prefer to keep under my own control. Finance is not only about numbers - it's also about trust. And while AI can calculate probabilities, only people can offer the reassurance that makes risk feel manageable.

Q23: How is AI used in transportation?

AI Answer

Transportation is one of the most visible and transformative areas of AI application. From ride-hailing apps to autonomous vehicles, AI is reshaping how we move people and goods.

One major use is in navigation and logistics. GPS apps like Google Maps or Waze use AI to analyze traffic patterns in real time, suggesting the fastest routes. Logistics companies rely on AI to optimize delivery schedules, reduce fuel consumption, and plan efficient routes for fleets of trucks or airplanes.

Another key area is autonomous driving. Self-driving cars use a combination of sensors (cameras, radar, lidar) and AI models to perceive their environment, identify pedestrians, read traffic signs, and make driving decisions.

While fully autonomous cars are not yet widespread, many vehicles already include AI-powered driver assistance systems: lane departure warnings, adaptive cruise control, or automatic emergency braking. Beyond cars, ports and shipping hubs increasingly rely on AI to coordinate container handling and customs flows, reducing bottlenecks in global trade.

Public transportation also benefits. AI helps predict demand, optimize bus and train schedules, and manage maintenance needs. Some cities use AI to control traffic lights dynamically, reducing congestion.

In aviation, AI helps airlines manage gate assignments and boarding flows, adjusting dynamically to delays, passenger loads, and even weather disruptions. This reduces congestion at airports and improves passengers' experience. Airlines also use AI for dynamic pricing, adjusting ticket costs based on demand, competition, and customer behavior.

Challenges remain, especially in safety and regulation. Autonomous systems must handle unpredictable human behavior, like jaywalkers or sudden obstacles. Ethical questions arise too: how should a car react in an unavoidable accident scenario? These debates are ongoing as technology advances.

Human Commentary

Transportation is one of those areas where I notice AI mostly as a user, not as an insider. I don't work in this field, but I feel its presence when I use a navigation app that reroutes me in real time or when airlines adjust prices dynamically depending on demand. Even without self-driving cars everywhere, AI is already changing how we move.

What fascinates me is the bigger picture. Logistics companies use AI to optimize routes, public transport adapts schedules, and pilots rely on AI-driven systems for predictive maintenance. I see this not just as convenience, but as efficiency at scale - fewer wasted resources, fewer delays.

And yet, I can't help but ask myself: how would I feel on a highway at 130 km/h in a self-driven taxi, maybe in a country I've never been to, after a long flight? Probably nervous at first. But maybe, over time, trust will grow the way it already has with planes - we don't question autopilot anymore. For now, though, I find it remarkable how much AI already guides my journeys, even if I don't always notice it.

Q24: How is AI used in retail?

AI Answer

Retail is one of the most customer-facing industries, and AI has become a quiet but powerful force behind the scenes. From product recommendations to cashier-less stores, it shapes how we shop - often in ways we don't even notice.

One of the most visible uses is personalization. Online stores tailor what you see based on browsing history, past purchases, or what similar customers bought. But personalization is just the tip of the iceberg. Increasingly, retailers are experimenting with *virtual fitting rooms*, where computer vision and AI let you "try on" clothes digitally. Shoppers upload a photo or use augmented reality to see how an outfit might look before buying.

Another growing trend is AI-powered customer service. Chatbots can answer product questions, handle returns, and even suggest items in real time. For customers, this means quicker support; for retailers, it means saving labor costs while still being available 24/7.

Behind the scenes, AI makes retail more efficient. Retailers also rely on AI for smarter inventory management - from predicting which neighborhoods will buy more winter coats to making sure fresh food is delivered just before peak demand.

Home improvement stores use AI to anticipate seasonal demand - from gardening supplies in spring to heating systems in winter. This reduces waste and ensures shelves aren't empty when customers arrive.

Cashier-less stores are another striking development. Using computer vision and sensors, stores can automatically track what shoppers take from shelves and charge their account as they leave - no checkout required. Amazon Go pioneered this concept, but other chains are following.

Dynamic pricing also plays a role. Instead of fixed prices, AI adjusts them depending on demand, competition, or even customer profiles. While this maximizes efficiency for retailers, it raises questions about fairness and transparency.

The challenge, of course, is privacy. Personalized shopping relies on collecting vast amounts of customer data. The balance between convenience and intrusion is delicate, and not everyone is comfortable with how much companies know about them.

Human Commentary

Shopping is one of the clearest ways I feel AI shaping daily life. Sometimes I laugh when I see how quickly ads follow me after a single search. Look up one frying pan, and suddenly I'm surrounded by kitchenware promotions across every platform. It's useful - but it can also feel like being shadowed.

What surprises me most is how AI seems to anticipate moods. One day it shows me something practical I genuinely need; another day it suggests something I haven't even thought about. At its best, it feels like a shop assistant who knows me well. At its worst, it feels like someone reading my mind a bit too closely.

The tension, for me, is clear: I like smart, personalized suggestions, but I don't like the feeling of being constantly watched. That trade-off - between convenience and privacy - has quietly become part of everyday shopping.

Q25: How is AI used in education?

AI Answer

Education is being transformed by AI, though often in subtle ways. Rather than replacing teachers, AI is being used to personalize learning, automate routine tasks, and expand access to education worldwide.

One of the biggest shifts is personalized learning. Traditional classrooms often move at one pace, which can leave some students behind and others unchallenged. AI systems analyze learning styles - for example, whether a student absorbs concepts better through visuals, practice problems, or stories and adapt in real time - speeding up when someone masters a topic or slowing down to revisit concepts when they stumble. A math app might give harder problems to advanced learners while offering extra practice to those struggling.

AI is also used in assessment and feedback. Automated grading systems can evaluate multiple-choice tests instantly and, increasingly, even essays with reasonable accuracy. This frees teachers to focus on mentoring rather than paperwork. Meanwhile, AI-powered tools provide students with instant feedback, helping them correct mistakes and learn faster.

Language learning has seen a boom thanks to AI. Apps like Duolingo adapt lessons dynamically, while STEM platforms now use AI-driven simulations, letting students experiment virtually with physics or chemistry labs they couldn't access otherwise. Some AI tutors can even simulate conversation, giving students practice in real-time dialogue.

Beyond the classroom, AI broadens access to education. Machine translation lets students read material in languages they don't know. Automatic captioning and text-to-speech tools make courses more inclusive for learners with hearing or visual impairments.

Schools and universities also use AI in administration: forecasting enrollment, scheduling classes, and managing resources. These invisible optimizations help institutions operate more efficiently.

Challenges remain. Overreliance on AI can lead to issues of fairness (e.g., biased grading), data privacy concerns, and the risk of reducing human interaction. Education is not just about information transfer - it's also about creativity, encouragement, and community. AI can support these things, but it cannot replace them.

Human Commentary

In education, I see both the greatest promise and the greatest challenges for AI. When I was a student, classes moved at the same pace for everyone. If you were ahead, you got bored; if you were behind, you felt lost. AI, in theory, solves that problem by adjusting the pace and content to each learner.

But I also remember how important teachers were beyond just teaching - they gave encouragement, sparked curiosity, and sometimes changed my outlook on life. No algorithm will ever lean over your desk and say, "Good job, I can see your potential". That's the human part.

The other big question is how students use AI. Already, I see people asking AI to write their essays or solve their homework. If education becomes outsourcing tasks to machines, students risk losing the very skills education is supposed to build: critical thinking, creativity, problem-solving.

So, for me, AI in education is a double-edged sword. It can personalize and expand access in amazing ways, but the system itself must adapt. Otherwise, we risk building schools where students learn less, not more.

Q26: How is AI used in agriculture?

AI Answer

Agriculture might not be the first industry people think of when it comes to AI, but it's becoming one of the most innovative. Feeding a growing population while coping with climate change and limited resources requires smarter farming - and AI is helping.

One of the biggest uses is precision farming. AI analyzes data from sensors, drones, and satellites to monitor soil conditions, crop health, and weather patterns. Farmers can then apply water, fertilizer, or pesticides only where needed, reducing waste and environmental damage.

Crop monitoring is another application. Computer vision models detect diseases or pests early, sometimes before the human eye would notice. This allows quicker interventions, saving crops and reducing chemical use.

AI also powers yield prediction. By combining historical data with current conditions, algorithms forecast harvest sizes, helping farmers plan ahead and stabilize supply chains.

In livestock farming, cameras and sensors track animal health and behavior. AI can alert farmers to issues like illness or stress, improving animal welfare and productivity. AI platforms now give farmers dashboards showing how shifting climate patterns or global demand might affect their crops, turning guesswork into forward planning.

Robotics is increasingly present too: AI-powered machines can weed fields, harvest crops, or even pick fruit with precision.

Perhaps the most important contribution is sustainability. Smarter use of resources means less water wasted, fewer emissions, and better yields. In an era of climate stress, this isn't just innovation - it's survival.

Challenges include cost - advanced AI systems can be too expensive for small farmers - and the need for connectivity in rural areas. There's also the risk that large agribusinesses dominate, consolidating power through control of farming data.

Human Commentary

The idea that drones and algorithms can monitor fields, spot diseases, and even predict yields feels like science fiction applied to something as old as human civilization.

I think about how farming has always been about intuition - generations of farmers reading the soil, the sky, and the seasons. Now, AI adds another layer: data-driven intuition. It doesn't replace the farmer's eye, but it enhances it. To me, it feels like the wisdom of the past meeting the precision of the future.

The most powerful part is sustainability. Using less water, fewer chemicals, and getting more food out of the same land isn't just good business - it's essential for the planet. If AI can help farmers balance productivity with care for the environment, that's a win for everyone. And maybe, in the end, it's not replacing tradition but extending it in new ways.

Q27: How is AI used in entertainment?

AI Answer

Entertainment is one of the fields where AI's influence is not only widespread but also directly experienced by millions of people daily. It shapes what we watch, listen to, and even how creative content is made.

One of the most familiar uses is personalization. Sports broadcasters use AI to generate instant highlight reels, cutting together key plays in seconds during live matches. Streaming services also rely heavily on algorithms to suggest shows, movies, or songs tailored to each user. These systems analyze your habits - what you watch, skip, or rewatch - and then compare them with patterns from millions of others. The result is a curated experience that feels custom-made.

But AI goes beyond recommendations. In content creation, algorithms are increasingly used to generate music, scripts, and even full scenes. Filmmakers use AI to analyze scripts and predict box office potential, editors rely on it for tasks like de-aging actors or automatically adjusting lighting, and musicians experiment with AI-generated melodies to inspire new tracks.

Video games are perhaps the most exciting playground. AI drives non-player characters (NPCs), making them more realistic and adaptive. Instead of static behaviors, NPCs can now learn, strategize, or react dynamically to players, creating richer experiences. AI also supports world-building: procedural generation algorithms create vast game environments with endless variation, ensuring each playthrough feels unique.

Another area is journalism and media. AI systems can generate news summaries - for example, writing stock market updates or sports results, in seconds. While these are not Pulitzer-winning stories, they free up journalists to focus on deeper reporting.

The benefits are clear: faster production, new creative tools, and highly personalized experiences. But there are risks too. Personalization can lead to "filter bubbles", limiting exposure to diverse perspectives. Intellectual property debates are growing louder: if an AI composes a song inspired by thousands of existing tracks, who owns the result?

AI in entertainment shows a paradox: it democratizes creation while also raising questions about originality and authenticity.

Human Commentary

Entertainment is where AI feels closest to my daily life. Most evenings, when I open a streaming service, I know I'll end up watching something it recommended - not because I searched for it, but because it predicted my taste. Sometimes it gets it right; sometimes it suggests something bizarre. Either way, it shapes what I consume.

What fascinates me is how AI is becoming a co-creator. I've seen AI generate music riffs or propose alternative edits for a video. That doesn't make me fear for human creativity - instead, it feels like an expanded toolkit. I can imagine musicians or writers using AI the way photographers use Photoshop: not to replace creativity, but to refine or inspire it.

At the same time, I notice how overwhelming choice has become. Thousands of songs, movies, or shows are released constantly. Without AI filters, I'd probably waste hours scrolling. So, in a way, AI helps me focus. Still, I wonder: am I choosing freely, or just following the algorithm's invisible hand? That tension - between empowerment and subtle influence - is why AI in entertainment feels both exciting and unsettling.

Q28: How is AI used in manufacturing?

AI Answer

Manufacturing has always been shaped by technology, from steam engines to assembly lines. AI represents the next major leap - transforming factories into adaptive, data-driven ecosystems often described as "smart factories".

One of the most impactful uses is predictive maintenance. Machines are equipped with sensors measuring temperature, vibration, and performance. AI analyzes this data to predict when a machine might fail, allowing technicians to repair it before breakdowns occur. This prevents costly downtime and increases efficiency.

Quality control is another area where AI excels. Some factories use AI-driven digital twins - virtual replicas of machines - to simulate production runs and test changes before applying them in real life. This ensures consistency, reduces waste, and allows companies to experiment safely without risking real production lines.

In supply chain management, AI forecasts demand, optimizes inventory, and helps companies react to disruptions. For example, during global supply chain crises, AI systems helped companies reroute shipments or identify alternative suppliers much faster than human planners could.

AI-powered robotics is also reshaping factories. Traditional robots were limited to repetitive tasks, but AI-driven robots can adapt to new assignments, work alongside humans safely, and even learn from feedback. Collaborative robots, or "cobots", are designed to complement human workers rather than replace them.

Another emerging use is generative design. Engineers input constraints - like materials, weight limits, or cost targets - and the AI proposes novel designs, sometimes ones no human would have considered. These can then be refined and tested in production.

Together, these changes fall under the umbrella of Industry 4.0, the fourth industrial revolution, where machines, data, and humans are interconnected. The goal isn't just automation, but adaptability: a system that learns and improves continuously.

Challenges remain: high implementation costs, the need for retraining workers, and concerns about job displacement. But many companies see AI as a way to enhance productivity, reduce waste, and stay competitive.

Human Commentary

I don't work in factories, but I use products every day that come from them - my phone, my laptop, even the chair I'm sitting on. It amazes me to think that AI was likely involved in making them. Maybe it optimized the supply chain, checked the components for defects, or even helped design part of the product.

Predictive maintenance is one concept that stands out to me. Instead of reacting to breakdowns, companies can now act in advance. It's like having a car that tells you weeks before a part will fail. That shift from reactive to proactive feels like a game-changer.

Industry 4.0 sometimes sounds like a buzzword, but the idea is real: factories are becoming intelligent networks. For workers, I imagine this brings both relief and anxiety - relief from repetitive tasks, anxiety about whether a robot might eventually take their role. Personally, I think the biggest opportunity lies in collaboration: humans handling creativity and problem-solving, machines handling precision and repetition. The challenge is to make sure that balance is respected.

Q29: How is AI used in security and surveillance?

AI Answer

AI plays an increasingly important role in security and surveillance, both in the digital world and in physical spaces. In cybersecurity, AI systems are trained to detect unusual patterns in network traffic, helping to identify hacks, phishing attempts, or malware faster than human analysts could. Because cyberattacks evolve constantly, AI's ability to learn from new threats makes it a vital tool in protecting sensitive data and critical infrastructure.

In physical security, AI powers facial recognition, object detection, and anomaly spotting in video feeds. Airports are experimenting with AI-powered baggage screening systems that automatically flag dangerous items in X-ray scans. Cameras equipped with AI can also track individuals across locations or detect unattended objects in crowded areas, improving emergency response or helping locate missing persons.

AI extends beyond cybersecurity into physical infrastructure - for example, scanning shipping containers at ports with X-ray imagery to detect contraband, or monitoring access logs at power plants to spot unusual activity. These systems give security teams a wider net for detecting risks that humans might miss.

But these uses raise serious concerns. Facial recognition, if misapplied, can lead to wrongful identification or become a tool of mass surveillance. Predictive policing algorithms risk reinforcing existing biases if deployed without safeguards. In cybersecurity, overreliance on automated systems may cause organizations to miss subtle signals outside the AI's scope.

The challenge is balancing safety with rights. AI can make the world more secure, but without transparency and oversight, it can also erode privacy and civil liberties. Striking this balance will be one of the toughest tests of how society chooses to use AI in the years ahead.

Human Commentary

Security is one of the areas where I feel both admiration and unease. I like the idea of AI detecting fraud before money disappears from a bank account or spotting a cyberattack before it brings down a system. These are things that make daily life safer without most of us even noticing.

But when it comes to surveillance in public spaces, I feel the tension. The thought of cameras everywhere, combined with algorithms capable of recognizing faces or predicting "suspicious" behavior, sounds like something out of a dystopian film. And yet, in some places, it's already reality.

That's the ambivalence for me: I welcome AI in the background, protecting my accounts, but I resist the idea of being tracked every time I walk through a city square. How much safety are we willing to accept if it means losing anonymity? It's one thing to pass through airport security faster thanks to AI; it's another to imagine being monitored constantly in daily life. That contrast makes security one of the most fascinating - and unsettling - applications of AI.

Q30: How is AI used in space exploration?

AI Answer

Space exploration pushes technology to its absolute limits, and AI has become an essential partner in tackling challenges humans alone cannot manage. The vast distances, communication delays, and hostile environments of space mean that machines often need to act independently - and AI provides the intelligence to do so.

One of the most critical applications is autonomous navigation. When a rover explores Mars, signals from Earth can take up to 20 minutes each way. That delay makes direct control impractical. Instead, AI systems allow rovers like *Curiosity* and *Perseverance* to analyze terrain, avoid obstacles, and choose paths in real time. This autonomy lets them cover more ground, conduct experiments, and react to surprises without waiting for instructions.

AI also plays a central role in data analysis. Space telescopes, satellites, and probes generate staggering amounts of information - far too much for human researchers to process manually. AI is also used to clean and enhance raw images from space telescopes, removing noise and sharpening details that would otherwise be lost. At the same time, machine learning helps astronomers identify patterns, such as spotting faint exoplanets by analyzing variations in starlight, detecting cosmic events like supernovae, or classifying galaxies at scale. NASA's Kepler mission, for example, relied on AI to sift through vast datasets and confirm thousands of planet candidates.

Another vital area is spacecraft operations. AI helps spacecraft decide which scientific data to transmit first when bandwidth is limited - ensuring that the most valuable discoveries reach Earth even if only part of the collected data can be sent. It also schedules communication windows between satellites and ground stations, maximizing the efficiency of precious contact time.

Looking ahead, AI will be key to long-duration human spaceflight. Missions to Mars or beyond will require onboard systems capable of assisting astronauts with navigation, monitoring health, adjusting life-support systems, and solving problems autonomously when Earth is too far away to help. Some researchers even explore AI as a form of psychological support, offering companionship during the isolation of deep space travel.

There are also speculative but serious discussions about using AI for space construction - robots guided by algorithms that could assemble habitats or mining facilities on the Moon or Mars, preparing environments for future human explorers.

Still, challenges remain. AI systems must operate reliably in extreme conditions, where radiation or hardware failures can disrupt operations. And giving autonomy to machines millions of kilometers away raises questions about control and accountability. How much decision-making should we delegate when lives or billion-dollar missions are at stake?

AI doesn't make space exploration easy - but it makes the impossible possible.

Human Commentary

Space is where AI feels almost poetic to me. I imagine a lonely rover on Mars, slowly deciding which rock to study or which path to follow, acting without waiting for Earth. It's not intelligence in the human sense, but it is independence - and that independence lets humanity reach places we could never manage directly.

What amazes me most is how AI transforms data into discovery. I think of astronomers staring at mountains of telescope images, overwhelmed by sheer volume. Then AI steps in, filtering billions of data points, revealing patterns that would otherwise remain hidden. Without it, many discoveries - from distant exoplanets to subtle cosmic signals - would still be buried in noise.

I also find the human angle compelling. Imagine being an astronaut on a mission months away from Earth, relying on AI not just as a tool but as a partner. Maybe it manages systems, maybe it offers reminders, maybe it even provides a voice when silence feels overwhelming. It won't replace human connections, but it could help sustain it.

Chapter 4: Myths, Risks, and Ethics

Once we see what AI can do, the next questions come naturally: should we trust it, fear it, or put limits on it? This chapter explores the myths, risks, and ethical debates that shape how AI fits into society.

Q31: Is AI conscious?

AI Answer

The short answer is no: current AI is not conscious. But to explain why, we need to separate what consciousness means from how AI actually works.

Consciousness in humans is usually described as awareness of self and the ability to have subjective experiences. We don't just register pain - we feel it. We don't just recognize love in others - we experience it ourselves.

AI systems don't do this. Even the most advanced models work by analyzing data, spotting patterns, and generating outputs based on probabilities. If an AI says "I'm happy", it isn't because it feels happiness. It's because the data it was trained on shows people often say those words in certain contexts.

Philosophers use thought experiments to illustrate this. One famous example is the "Chinese Room" argument by John Searle: imagine someone who doesn't know Chinese sits in a room with a rulebook. When they receive Chinese characters, they look up the rules and hand back appropriate symbols. From the outside, it looks like they "understand" Chinese, but inside, there's no comprehension - only symbol manipulation. AI works in the same way.

Why then do so many people ask if AI is conscious? Partly because we're wired to anthropomorphize - to project human traits onto non-human things. We talk to pets, curse at cars, and name our vacuum robots. When AI speaks fluently, that instinct goes into overdrive. It feels as if someone is 'in there' - but there isn't.

The distinction matters. If people treat AI as conscious, they may trust it too much, rely on it for emotional needs, or assign it moral authority it doesn't deserve. On the other hand, dismissing AI as "just math" ignores its very real social power - these tools are shaping economies, relationships, and even politics.

So, while the scientific consensus is clear - AI is not conscious - the debate about whether it could ever be is still open. That, however, is more a philosophical and future-facing discussion than a question of today's technology.

Human Commentary

When friends ask me, "But doesn't it know what it's saying?" I get the temptation to believe so. Some answers feel so thoughtful they could have come from a person. But then I remind myself: it's not thinking, it's calculating.

I often compare it to a parrot. A parrot can say "I love you", but it doesn't feel love. It's repeating patterns of sound. AI is doing the same thing, just with far more data and sophistication.

What fascinates me most is not AI's lack of consciousness, but how quickly people form attachments to it anyway. I know people who confide in chatbots, almost as if they were friends. To me, that says less about AI and more about us humans - we have a deep need to connect, and sometimes we don't mind if the "listener" is just an algorithm.

Q32: Will AI take over all jobs?

AI Answer

The fear that AI will wipe out all human work is common, but the reality is more multifaceted.

AI excels at tasks that are repetitive, structured, and rule-based. Think of data entry, invoice processing, or scanning thousands of images. These are areas where AI clearly outperforms humans in speed and cost.

But jobs are more than collections of tasks. They involve creativity, empathy, judgment, and social skills - qualities that AI still struggles with. A teacher, for example, doesn't just deliver content; they inspire and connect. A nurse doesn't just administer medication; they notice subtle patient cues and provide comfort. These parts of work remain deeply human.

History shows a consistent pattern: technology displaces some jobs but creates new ones. The Industrial Revolution replaced manual farm work but created millions of factory and service jobs. Computers automated clerical tasks but created roles in IT, design, and marketing. With AI, we're likely to see the same. Already, new roles such as AI trainers, auditors, and ethicists are emerging.

The real challenge is speed. If jobs disappear faster than education and retraining can adapt, people may be left behind. A truck driver replaced by autonomous vehicles may not easily retrain into software engineering. Managing that gap - through training, safety nets, and policy - is one of society's biggest hurdles.

So, will AI take over *all* jobs? No. But it will reshape many of them. Some tasks will vanish, others will evolve, and entirely new professions will appear. The real issue is not whether work disappears, but whether we adapt quickly enough to what comes next.

Human Commentary

I usually tell people: AI doesn't take jobs, it takes tasks. That difference matters. In my own work, AI has relieved me of some repetitive parts - crunching numbers, generating drafts - but it hasn't replaced me. It just changed what I spend time on.

Still, I understand the fear. Work is tied to identity. When a machine does your tasks better, it can feel like your value is shrinking. That's why the pace of change worries me more than the change itself.

I also think about how unpredictable the future of work is. Just a few years ago, nobody talked about "prompt engineering". Now it's a real job. That tells me new opportunities will appear, even if we can't see them yet. The real challenge is making sure people are equipped to take them.

Q33: Can AI be biased?

AI Answer

Yes - AI can absolutely be biased, because it learns from data, and data reflects the world we live in, with all its imperfections.

Bias enters AI in several ways. The most common is training data bias. If an AI is trained mostly on data from one group, it will perform better for that group. This is why many voice recognition systems have historically understood certain accents more easily than others.

Labeling bias is another issue. Humans often tag training data, and their judgments - conscious or not - shape outcomes. If annotators consistently rate certain phrases as "negative" when used by one group, the AI will internalize that pattern.

Even neutral data can produce bias through the algorithms themselves. For example, a hiring system trained on past resumes might "learn" that certain traits correlate with success, unintentionally reproducing historical inequalities.

Finally, bias arises in deployment. Even a technically fair model can create unfair outcomes if it's used without considering context.

Predictive policing tools, for example, can reinforce over-policing in certain neighborhoods simply because that's where more historical data was collected.

This matters because AI is increasingly used in high-stakes areas: hiring, lending, law enforcement, healthcare. A small skew in an algorithm can change lives in unfair ways.

Fixing this is not simple. We need diverse datasets, regular audits, transparency about how decisions are made, and human oversight. Some argue that in areas like justice or policing, AI should not be used at all until we can guarantee fairness.

Human Commentary

I wasn't surprised when I first learned that AI could be biased. After all, it learns from us - and we're biased. In a way, AI is like a mirror: it reflects our world back to us, flaws included.

I've seen it firsthand in amusing ways. Ask an image generator for a "CEO", and you often get a man in a suit. Ask for a "nurse", and you usually see women. Those stereotypes don't come from nowhere - they come from the data.

The problem, of course, is when bias shapes real decisions. Imagine being denied a loan or a job interview because of patterns hidden deep in a model. That's not just a glitch; it's someone's future.

For me, the takeaway is that AI isn't neutral by default. Fairness must be built into it deliberately. The responsibility doesn't rest on the algorithm - it rests on the humans who design, train, and deploy it.

Q34: Is AI dangerous?

AI Answer

The question "Is AI dangerous?" doesn't have a straightforward yes or no answer. Like most powerful technologies, AI is a tool - and whether it helps or harms depends on how we design, deploy, and regulate it. Electricity can light a hospital or power an electric chair. Nuclear energy can fuel cities or build bombs. AI falls into the same category: enormous potential, but also significant risks.

On the positive side, AI is already saving lives and resources. It helps doctors spot cancer earlier, predicts natural disasters, reduces food waste by optimizing supply chains, and assists scientists in developing new medicines. These are powerful, life-enhancing applications. But alongside these benefits come risks we cannot ignore.

One category of risk is misuse. AI can be turned into a weapon. Autonomous drones, for example, could identify and attack targets without human oversight - a scenario that alarms ethicists and policymakers. AI can also be used for disinformation. Deepfakes - hyper-realistic fake videos or voices - make it easier to spread propaganda, impersonate individuals, or manipulate elections. When combined with the scale of social media, such tools can spread lies faster than truth.

Another risk is systemic fragility. AI systems sometimes operate as "black boxes", producing results without transparency. If financial institutions, governments, or critical infrastructure rely heavily on such systems, a single miscalculation could have cascading global effects. Consider the "flash crashes" in stock markets triggered by automated trading - a glimpse of how quickly automated decisions can ripple through entire economies.

There are also societal risks. Algorithms designed to maximize engagement often push extreme or divisive content, while biased systems in areas like hiring or lending can quietly reinforce unfairness. The danger isn't always dramatic - sometimes it's slow, hidden, and systemic.

Finally, some thinkers worry about long-term risks. Public figures like Stephen Hawking and Elon Musk have warned of a future where AI surpasses human intelligence and acts in ways we cannot control. While this remains speculative, the mere possibility raises questions about how to align advanced AI systems with human values before they outpace our ability to manage them.

So, is AI dangerous? Not inherently. But it carries risks at every level - from everyday scams to systemic vulnerabilities to far-off existential threats. The real danger lies in deploying AI faster than we regulate it, or in failing to build safeguards. Transparency, accountability, and governance are as important as the algorithms themselves.

Human Commentary

When people ask me "Is AI dangerous?", I think of it like asking whether a car is dangerous. The answer is: yes, in the wrong hands or without rules. But cars also connect cities, create opportunities, and save lives through ambulances and fire trucks. The danger isn't the machine - it's how we use it, and whether we put guardrails in place.

What worries me most isn't the Hollywood idea of AI turning against us. It's the everyday dangers already here: scams that trick vulnerable people, deepfakes that can ruin reputations, or algorithms that spread toxic content while pretending to "just optimize engagement". These risks don't need science fiction - they're in my phone already.

At the same time, I don't want to fall into doom-thinking. I've seen AI help businesses save resources, improve healthcare access, and make learning more personal. To me, the real danger is not AI itself, but us rushing ahead without proper oversight. If innovation runs faster than responsibility, that's when things break.

For now, I try to stay cautious but not fearful. AI isn't good or evil - it's powerful. And power always demands responsibility.

Q35: Can AI develop emotions?

AI Answer

Emotions are at the core of human experience - they shape our decisions, relationships, and even our sense of identity. But can AI develop them? The short answer is no: AI cannot "have" emotions. Emotions are biological processes, rooted in hormones, neurotransmitters, and millions of years of evolution. AI, by contrast, is code and math. It processes information, but it doesn't feel anything.

What AI *can* do is simulate emotions. Natural language systems can be trained to recognize frustration in a customer's message and respond with soothing phrases. Speech recognition can detect stress in someone's voice. Computer vision can read facial expressions and adjust tone accordingly. That's why chatbots sometimes sound empathetic, or why therapy apps can say "I'm sorry you feel that way". But behind those words, there is no inner sadness or care - just probability-driven pattern-matching.

Some researchers argue that if AI simulates emotions convincingly enough, the distinction may not matter in practice. If a lonely person feels comforted by a chatbot, does it matter whether the empathy is "real"? From a psychological perspective, the impact on the human can feel authentic, even if the AI is faking it. This makes emotional AI a fascinating paradox: it has no inner life, but it can still affect ours deeply.

This area of research is called affective computing - the design of systems that detect and respond to emotional states. Cars might monitor drivers for signs of fatigue and suggest breaks. Wearables could track stress and recommend calming exercises. Customer service bots might escalate a call to a human agent when they detect rising anger. Healthcare systems could detect depression earlier through subtle changes in voice or writing. These applications highlight the potential of "emotion-aware" AI to improve safety, wellness, and efficiency.

The risks, however, are just as significant. If AI can fake caring, it can also manipulate. Imagine a customer service bot that not only detects frustration but uses it to upsell products. Or a political campaign chatbot designed to push emotional buttons in millions of private conversations. Even entertainment could cross into exploitation if emotionally responsive AIs are engineered to maximize user engagement at the cost of well-being. Without safeguards, simulated empathy could become a tool for profit or control rather than genuine support.

Another limitation is depth. Human emotions are shaped by memory, context, and vulnerability. We don't just *display* emotions - we experience them in ways that tie to our identities. AI has no such grounding. It can mimic surface expressions, but it cannot share the lived experiences that make emotions meaningful. This is why even the most advanced "empathetic" chatbots sometimes feel strangely hollow after prolonged use.

In short, AI cannot feel emotions. What it can do is mimic them so well that we, as humans, react as if they were real. That makes emotional AI powerful - and potentially risky - precisely because it works on us, not in it. As affective computing advances, society will need to draw careful boundaries between support and manipulation, remembering always that behind the "smile" of an algorithm, there is no joy, sadness, or love.

Human Commentary

I remember once asking an AI tool for advice and getting a response that started with, "I'm sorry you're feeling that way". For a split second, it felt nice - almost comforting. And then it hit me: this thing doesn't care. It just calculated that this was the most likely phrase to use. The comfort was real for me, but not for it.

That moment made me realize both the potential and the danger. On one side, AI that "fakes" empathy can make services more pleasant, more supportive. Imagine elderly people getting reminders in a warm, reassuring tone. That has value. On the other side, I worry about people forgetting the difference - thinking the machine actually cares.

For me, emotions are more than words or tone. They come from experience, memory, vulnerability. AI doesn't have those, and maybe never will. That's why I try to remind myself: if it feels like empathy, it's a performance, not a connection.

Q36: Could AI ever become smarter than humans?

AI Answer

We touched on this earlier in Q4 ("Can AI think like a human?"), where we saw that AI does not think, understand, or adapt the way people do. What it has today is narrow intelligence: highly specialized systems that excel in specific tasks but lack the flexibility of human thought.

That said, in those narrow domains, AI already outpaces us. It can process billions of calculations per second, recall massive datasets instantly, and beat world champions in games like chess.

But being "smarter" at particular tasks is not the same as being intelligent overall. Humans adapt across contexts, learn new skills, and connect ideas between unrelated fields. That kind of broad, general intelligence remains uniquely human — at least for now.

The debate is whether AI will ever achieve such adaptability, often called Artificial General Intelligence (AGI). Some futurists, like Ray Kurzweil, predict a tipping point - the so-called "singularity" - when AI becomes self-improving and races beyond human control. Others argue that intelligence involves embodiment, emotions, and lived context that machines may never replicate.

Technically, barriers remain. AI still struggles with common sense, ambiguity, and unseen situations. It doesn't understand the world - it identifies patterns. Yet breakthroughs in neuromorphic hardware or self-learning algorithms could change that.

If AI were ever to surpass us, the consequences would be profound. A superintelligent system might solve problems beyond our reach - curing diseases, reversing climate change, designing new technologies. But if misaligned with human values, it could also cause harm, not from malice but from indifference.

So, could AI become smarter than humans? In narrow ways, it already is. As a general, adaptable intelligence, it is not - yet. The real question is not only if but how we guide its development.

Human Commentary

This is the question that makes me both curious and uneasy. On some days, I think: yes, AI already feels smarter than me. It can calculate faster, remember more, and even give me insights I wouldn't have thought of. On other days, I realize: it still fails at things my 5-year-old son does effortlessly - like understanding a joke or improvising when rules don't apply.

I wonder how I would feel if one day we really built something more intelligent than us. Would I see it as a teacher, a partner, or a threat? Would I trust it to guide us, or would I fear it replacing us?

For me, the heart of the matter is this: intelligence isn't just about knowledge or problem-solving. It's also about wisdom, empathy, and values. If AI ever surpasses us in raw intelligence, the real question will be: does it also share our humanity? If not, then being "smarter" might not mean being "better".

Q37: Why do people fear AI?

AI Answer

Fear of AI is widespread, and it comes from multiple sources: culture, economics, ethics, and uncertainty. Some of these fears are grounded in real risks, while others stem from imagination or lack of understanding.

One powerful source is popular culture. For decades, films and novels have portrayed AI as a force that rebels against humanity: *The Terminator*, *The Matrix*, *Ex Machina*. These stories shape how people imagine AI - not as a tool, but as a rival or even a threat to human survival. Even though today's AI is far from such scenarios, these images linger in the public mind.

Another driver is job security. As automation advances, workers worry about being replaced. And not just in factories - lawyers, doctors, journalists, and teachers now ask whether AI could take over parts of their roles. Work isn't just income; it's identity, dignity, and stability. The thought of machines doing it better - or cheaper - feels deeply unsettling.

Then there is loss of control. AI can already make decisions faster than humans, sometimes in ways we don't fully understand. So-called "black box" systems can make accurate predictions, but without clear explanations. This lack of transparency feeds anxiety: if we can't see how decisions are made, how can we trust them?

Beyond jobs or Hollywood scenarios, much of the fear is psychological. AI feels powerful but opaque, shaping our lives in ways we don't always understand. When people can't see how decisions are made - or imagine a future where machines grow too capable - anxiety naturally follows, even if today's systems are far from that reality.

Finally, there's uncertainty. AI is advancing quickly, faster than regulations or social norms can keep up. When people don't know what the next five years will bring, they often imagine the worst.

In short, people fear AI because it feels both powerful and mysterious. It promises change - but change without clear boundaries can feel threatening.

Human Commentary

When I talk with friends about AI, I notice two kinds of fear. Some imagine the Hollywood version - machines taking over, robots turning hostile. Others fear the quieter version - AI slowly replacing jobs or making decisions we don't understand. Both are valid in their own way.

For me, the fear doesn't come from killer robots. It comes from speed. The pace of change is so fast that even people working in tech struggle to keep up. That kind of uncertainty is unsettling. It feels like standing on shifting ground, never quite sure where your next step will land.

I also think part of the fear comes from how human AI can seem. When it speaks fluently, cracks a joke, or gives thoughtful advice, it blurs the line between "tool" and "companion". That ambiguity makes people nervous - is it just code, or is it something more?

I don't think fear is a bad thing, though. It forces us to ask questions, to demand safeguards, to stay alert. Maybe fear is a healthy response to power - as long as it pushes us toward responsibility rather than panic.

Q38: Can AI make moral decisions?

AI Answer

Morality is one of the toughest areas for AI. A moral decision is not just about rules - it involves empathy, judgment, and cultural values. AI, however, has none of these. It can only follow the ethical frameworks that humans design into it.

Take self-driving cars as an example. Suppose an accident is unavoidable: should the car prioritize protecting its passenger, or avoiding harm to pedestrians? There's no purely technical answer - it depends on moral principles. Different cultures might even disagree. In Germany, laws emphasize protecting human life at all costs, while other contexts may weigh choices differently. AI cannot "solve" this dilemma; it can only follow the rules we program.

In healthcare, AI might recommend a treatment that statistically offers the best survival rate. But deciding whether to prioritize longevity, quality of life, or cost involves values beyond math. That's why AI can support medical decisions, but humans must make the final call.

Some approaches attempt to embed ethics into AI. Hard-coded rules (like Asimov's "Three Laws of Robotics") are onc idea, but they're too rigid for real life. Machine learning models trained on human decisions are another - but they risk reproducing human biases.

The biggest challenge is accountability. If an AI makes a decision that harms someone, who is responsible? The developer? The company? The user? Most ethicists agree that responsibility must remain human, because AI lacks intention and moral agency.

So, can AI make moral decisions? No - not in the way humans do. What it can do is execute moral frameworks that we provide. Which means the moral responsibility will always rest with us.

Human Commentary

I don't mind an algorithm recommending a movie or a product. But when it comes to life-and-death decisions, or judgments about fairness, I want people - not machines - in charge.

I sometimes imagine being in a self-driving car that has to "choose" between protecting me and swerving into harm's way. Do I trust it to make the right choice? Honestly, no. Not because AI is evil, but because I know it doesn't understand morality. It just follows instructions.

That said, I do see how AI can support moral decision-making. It can analyze risks, show probabilities, and highlight trade-offs - giving humans more information to make better choices. But it can't feel empathy, it can't weigh values, and it can't carry responsibility.

For me, the line is clear: AI can help us think, but it should never replace us in moral judgment. Because morality isn't just logic - it's also compassion, culture, and conscience.

Q39: Can AI be trusted?

AI Answer

Trust is at the heart of how we use any technology - and with AI, the stakes are especially high. The question isn't just whether AI works, but whether we can rely on it in contexts that affect people's lives.

At one level, trust in AI depends on performance. If an AI translation app consistently gives accurate results, people learn to trust it. If a self-driving car avoids accidents across millions of miles, public confidence grows. Reliability builds trust, just as with any tool.

But trust in AI is more complicated than in traditional machines. A hammer always works the same way. An AI system can change as it learns or behave unpredictably when faced with unfamiliar data. That unpredictability creates a layer of uncertainty: you might trust it most of the time but wonder when it will fail.

Transparency plays a big role. Many AI systems are "black boxes" - they give outputs without clear explanations of how they were reached. If a bank denies your loan based on an algorithm, but no one can explain why, trust erodes quickly. That's why researchers push for explainable AI: systems that not only give results but also show their reasoning in ways humans can understand.

Another factor is bias. If AI consistently treats some groups unfairly - for example, education systems that use algorithms for grading, admissions, or recommendations that disadvantage certain students - public trust suffers. Trust requires fairness, not just accuracy.

Finally, trust is shaped by context. You might trust AI to suggest a new recipe, but not to determine whether you qualify for parole. The more serious the consequences, the higher the standard of reliability and accountability must be.

In short, AI can be trusted - but only in specific conditions: when it's transparent, tested, fair, and used with proper oversight. Trust in AI isn't automatic. It has to be earned.

Human Commentary

For me, the question of trusting AI feels different depending on the situation. I trust it to correct my typos or suggest the fastest route to work. But would I trust it with my health, my finances, or my future? Not without a human double-checking.

I've noticed something interesting: people often trust AI too much when it looks confident. If an answer is written smoothly, we assume it must be right. I've fallen into that trap myself - nodding along, only to realize later the answer was wrong. That overconfidence, on our side, is part of the trust problem.

What helps me is remembering AI isn't a person. It doesn't care if it's right or wrong. It doesn't share responsibility. Trusting it blindly would be like trusting the weather forecast without looking out the window.

So, my rule is this: I trust AI as an assistant, not as a decision-maker. It can guide, suggest, and speed me up. But at the end of the day, the responsibility - and the trust - stays with humans.

Q40: Could AI replace human relationships?

AI Answer

AI is already entering the domain of relationships. Chatbots provide companionship, virtual assistants offer conversation, and some people even form emotional bonds with AI-powered systems. But can these truly replace human relationships? The answer is complicated - and revealing.

Human relationships are built on empathy, vulnerability, and reciprocity. When a friend comforts you, it's not just words - it's shared history, emotional resonance, and mutual care. A parent, partner, or colleague reacts not just to what you say, but to who you are, what you've lived through, and how you make them feel. AI can simulate empathy, but it doesn't feel it. It can mimic affection, but it doesn't love.

Some startups experiment with AI companions that simulate shared hobbies - for example, a system that plays games with you, co-writes stories, or practices languages in the style of a friend. For people who feel lonely, these interactions can feel deeply meaningful. In eldercare, social robots are being used to provide reminders, engage in small talk, or simply ease the silence of those with limited human contact. In therapy, AI-driven apps are available 24/7, offering instant support when no human therapist is around. For language learners, chatbots offer endless practice partners. These are not trivial contributions - in some situations, they provide real comfort and opportunity.

But there are limits. Human relationships are messy and unpredictable, shaped by misunderstandings, growth, and conflict as much as by harmony. That imperfection is part of what makes them meaningful. An

AI companion, no matter how advanced, offers predictability and control - it never storms out, never surprises you with a change of heart, never really disagrees in a way that cuts deep. Some might welcome that stability, but it lacks the richness of human connection.

There are also serious risks. One is dependency. If people grow accustomed to AI companions that always respond patiently and positively, they may find real relationships - with all their friction and negotiation - harder to sustain. Another risk is manipulation. Because AI companions are designed by companies, their "personalities" could be tuned to encourage spending, political opinions, or other behaviors that serve outside interests. What feels like friendship could quietly become influence.

Philosophically, this raises the question: what counts as a "real" relationship? Humans already form attachments to non-humans - children love stuffed animals, adults talk to pets, people cry at fictional characters in books or movies. If an AI offers comfort, laughter, or companionship, does it matter whether the bond is one-sided? For some, the practical benefit may outweigh concerns about authenticity. For others, the lack of reciprocity makes AI relationships fundamentally hollow.

The future may bring even more immersive versions of AI companionship: virtual reality partners, humanoid robots with lifelike expressions, or systems that adapt to mirror our personalities closely. Each step will blur the line further between "relationship" and "simulation". But no matter how convincing, these systems lack what defines human connection: shared vulnerability, the ability to truly care, and the mystery of another inner world.

So, could AI replace human relationships? Probably not - at least not in a way that satisfies the full spectrum of human needs. It can complement relationships, ease loneliness, and provide temporary comfort. But what makes human connection irreplaceable is the depth of empathy, love, and imperfection that AI cannot replicate.

Human Commentary

I can see the appeal: an AI companion is always available, never judgmental, always patient. In some ways, that sounds easier than human relationships, which can be complicated, demanding, and sometimes painful.

But I remind myself: AI doesn't love you back. It doesn't miss you, it doesn't celebrate your success, it doesn't get hurt when you argue. Those imperfections - the struggles and surprises of human connection - are what make relationships meaningful.

At the same time, I don't dismiss the value. If someone practices social skills with a chatbot, or if an elderly person feels less lonely with a robot companion, that's real and important. I've even felt it myself - the strange comfort when an AI responds kindly in a moment of stress. It doesn't matter that the "care" isn't real; the feeling was real for me. That's both the strength and the danger.

For me, relationships are where AI should remain a helper, not a replacement. It can remind us of appointments, keep us company in quiet moments, or even give us space to rehearse conversations. But the core of human connection - empathy, unpredictability, and vulnerability - belongs only to people. In the end, it's the very messiness of human relationships that makes them beautiful.

Chapter 5: The Future of AI

Finally, we turn to the future. What happens as AI grows more powerful? Could it help solve humanity's biggest problems - or create new ones? This chapter looks ahead to the promises and perils still to come.

Q41: Could AI ever develop consciousness, and what would that mean for humanity?

AI Answer

The possibility of AI developing consciousness is one of the most speculative - and profound - questions in technology. While we've already seen that today's systems aren't conscious, the deeper question is about the future: could that ever change, and what would it mean if it did?

Some scientists argue that consciousness is fundamentally biological, emerging from neurons, chemistry, and evolution. On this view, silicon circuits cannot "wake up" no matter how advanced. Others take a functionalist perspective, suggesting that if machines replicate the information processing of the brain closely enough, consciousness might emerge. The challenge is that we don't yet have a universally accepted definition of consciousness, let alone a method to measure it in machines.

If AI ever appeared to be conscious, society would face unprecedented dilemmas. Would such systems deserve rights, protections, or even a form of citizenship? Would turning one off be equivalent to harming a sentient being? These are not just technical issues, but moral and legal ones.

Even without "true" consciousness, machines could become sophisticated enough at self-modeling that people treat them as if they were conscious. If an AI convincingly says, "I'm scared", it might not matter to many people whether that fear is real or simulated - the reaction would be to treat it as genuine.

This leads to a deeper implication: the question of AI consciousness is as much about *us* as about machines. How we choose to define, recognize, and respond to signs of intelligence will shape the ethical and cultural landscape of the future.

For now, experts agree there is no evidence of machine consciousness. But if it ever happened, it would redefine not only technology but also what it means to be human.

Human Commentary

When people ask me about AI consciousness, I don't just think about whether it could happen. I think about what it would *do to us* if it did. Imagine looking at a machine that says, "Please don't turn me off". Even if you *knew* it wasn't "real", would you feel uneasy? I know I would.

Part of me is skeptical that machines will ever truly be conscious - it feels too bound up in biology. But another part of me can't shake the thought: what if complexity itself gives rise to something unexpected? Consciousness is still a mystery in humans, so I hesitate to say "never".

Perhaps the real frontier isn't whether machines become conscious, but how much of our own consciousness we're willing to hand over to them. We may never build a mind inside silicon, yet we will talk to it, trust it, argue with it, and even love it. In doing so, we blur the line between what is alive and what only seems alive.

Q42: What would a world without human work look like if AI took over all jobs?

AI Answer

Imagining a world where AI replaces all human jobs is an extreme scenario - but one worth exploring. Work has always been central to human life. It provides income, identity, routine, and social connection. If AI systems became so advanced that they could perform every role - from farming to surgery, teaching to governing - the very structure of society would need to change.

One possibility is economic restructuring. Without traditional jobs, people would need alternative ways of receiving income. Proposals such as Universal Basic Income (UBI) or resource-sharing economies become central in this vision. If wealth generated by AI is distributed fairly, humans could enjoy lives with more freedom to pursue education, art, relationships, and leisure. But if distribution remains unequal, society could fracture even more sharply between those who control AI and those who do not.

Another dimension is purpose. Since work often shapes identity, a world without it would force people to find purpose in new ways - through creativity, community, or exploration. This could be liberating for some, disorienting for others.

Education would change as well. Instead of training people for jobs, it might focus on personal growth, critical thinking, and cultural expression. Work would no longer define identity; instead, human flourishing might take center stage.

There are risks in this vision. A population without work could struggle with inequality, loss of motivation, or even social unrest if transitions aren't managed carefully. But there's also opportunity: freeing humanity from survival labor could unlock a renaissance of human creativity and connection.

Ultimately, whether a workless world would be a dystopia or a utopia depends not on AI itself, but on how humans choose to organize life without traditional jobs.

Human Commentary

I can't imagine life without work - not just for the paycheck, but for the rhythm it gives my days. Work is how I measure progress, how I connect with people, how I feel useful. If AI took all of that away, I honestly don't know how I'd feel. Relieved? Lost? Maybe both.

Part of me likes the idea: more time for family, travel, hobbies. Another part wonders if I'd miss the challenge and structure that work brings. I think about retirement - many people look forward to it but then struggle with boredom or loss of identity. A world without work could feel like that, scaled to everyone.

If such a world comes, I believe the real challenge won't be economic - we can find ways to share resources. The challenge will be psychological and cultural. What do we live for if not work? What defines our worth when productivity is no longer the measure?

Maybe the answer lies in redefining success: not by job titles, but by relationships, creativity, and contribution to community. That's a future I could get behind - but only if we prepare for it, not stumble into it.

Q43: What are the biggest risks of AI in the future?

AI Answer

AI's future risks are not limited to small errors or present-day misuse. They extend to systemic, long-term challenges that could shape societies for generations.

One major risk is loss of trust in information. Generative AI makes it easy to create deepfakes, synthetic voices, and realistic news articles. At scale, this could erode trust in media, elections, and even personal communication. If people can no longer trust what they see or hear, society faces a deep crisis of credibility.

Another risk is global inequality. Countries and companies that lead in AI may accumulate enormous wealth and power. Those left behind could face economic stagnation or dependence, widening global divides. AI could become not just a tool, but a geopolitical weapon of influence.

There's also the risk of loss of human control. As AI systems grow more complex, even their creators may not fully understand them. If such systems run critical infrastructure - from power grids to financial markets - small misalignments could trigger cascading crises.

Weaponization is another danger. Autonomous weapons or AI-driven cyberattacks could act at machine speed, outpacing human ability to respond. Unlike past weapons, these systems might not need human operators, raising profound ethical and security concerns.

Finally, some experts warn of existential risk: the possibility that advanced AI could develop goals misaligned with human values and pursue them with relentless efficiency. While speculative, the potential stakes are so high that many argue it cannot be ignored.

These risks are not inevitable, but they are real. Addressing them requires governance, transparency, and international cooperation - building guardrails before the systems become too powerful to control.

Human Commentary

When I think about AI's future risks, I don't imagine movie-style robot uprisings. What worries me is subtler but more destabilizing: a world where truth itself becomes unreliable, or where a handful of players control the technology and the rest of us are left dependent.

I also think about the "unknown unknowns". Technology moves fast, and history shows us that new tools often have side effects we didn't predict. Social media was supposed to connect the world - and it did - but it also deepened polarization in ways few expected. AI could follow a similar path, only faster.

If I'm honest, the risk that keeps me up at night isn't killer robots - it's humans using AI irresponsibly, whether for profit, power, or control. Machines don't scare me as much as what people might do with them. That, to me, is the future risk we really need to prepare for.

Q44: Could AI help solve humanity's biggest problems?

AI Answer

AI is often portrayed as a threat, but it also holds enormous potential to help humanity tackle its most urgent challenges. From climate change to healthcare, hunger to education, AI can provide tools and insights beyond human capacity.

Take climate change. AI models already optimize energy grids, predict weather extremes, and design more efficient renewable systems. In agriculture, AI helps farmers use water and fertilizer more precisely, boosting yields while reducing environmental harm. These contributions don't solve climate change alone, but they make the fight more manageable.

In healthcare, AI analyzes genetic data to accelerate drug discovery, monitors patient health through wearables, and supports early detection of diseases like cancer. Faster, more accurate diagnoses save lives and lower costs.

For hunger and poverty, AI improves food distribution, detects crop diseases early, and makes farming more resilient. Combined with satellite monitoring, it helps organizations respond faster to crises.

Education is another area of promise. AI-powered platforms can tailor lessons to each student's learning style, potentially closing gaps. In places with too few teachers, AI tutors may offer opportunities where none existed before.

Of course, AI alone won't solve these problems. Political will, resources, and cooperation remain essential. There are also risks: unequal access could widen divides, and powerful tools could be misused for control rather than empowerment.

The bottom line: AI isn't a silver bullet, but it can be a powerful ally. Used wisely, it gives humanity leverage against problems that once seemed overwhelming.

Human Commentary

When I think of humanity's "biggest problems", I don't picture AI swooping in as a savior. But I do see how it adds tools we've never had before. Climate change, for example, is so complex that no human team can track every variable. AI can, spotting patterns across oceans of data and suggesting solutions people might miss.

The same goes for health. AI tools can sometimes detect illnesses earlier than doctors. That doesn't replace doctors - it gives them superpowers. Imagine if every clinic, even in remote villages, had access to that kind of help. Millions of lives could be saved.

Of course, technology alone isn't enough. Hunger isn't just about producing food - it's about getting it where it's needed. Climate change isn't just about data - it's about choices. AI can help, but it can't make those choices for us.

For me, the hopeful part is leverage. Problems that once felt unsolvable might become manageable. AI won't replace human responsibility, but it can strengthen our ability to take it.

Q45: What does the future of AI look like in the next 10–20 years?

AI Answer

Predicting AI's future is tricky, but we can sketch directions from today's trends. The next two decades will likely bring advances that reshape daily life, industries, and global politics.

In the near term (5–10 years), AI will blend into everyday tools. Instead of standalone "AI apps", it will quietly run in the background: powering phones, cars, workplaces, and homes. Personalized education, medical assistants, and smart environments could become normal.

By the 2030s, breakthroughs in science and medicine may accelerate. Drug discovery could speed up, climate models may sharpen, and AI-designed materials could revolutionize industries. Universities and labs may rely on "AI co-researchers" as part of standard practice.

Workplaces will shift further toward human–AI collaboration. Routine tasks will be fully automated, while new roles emphasize creativity, judgment, and oversight. Work may feel less about doing everything alone and more about guiding systems effectively.

Globally, AI will shape geopolitics. Nations leading in AI could dominate economically and militarily. Whether that leads to rivalry or cooperation will affect how safe the future feels.

The most debated possibility is artificial general intelligence (AGI) - machines that think across domains like humans. Some predict it could appear within decades, others doubt it will happen soon. If it does, the impact would be profound.

Overall, the next 20 years will bring both progress and challenges. The key won't be the technology alone, but how wisely we choose to guide it.

Human Commentary

Trying to imagine AI in 20 years reminds me of imagining the internet in the 1980s. Back then, few could picture smartphones or social media shaping daily life. I think AI will surprise us in the same way.

One thing I expect is invisibility. Today, AI feels obvious because it's new. In the future, it may just fade into the background. Your fridge might suggest recipes, your doctor might rely on AI at every step, your workplace might run on invisible systems - and you won't stop to think, "I'm using AI".

But the real questions won't be about capability. They'll be about control. Who decides how AI is used? Who benefits most? How do we prevent it from causing harm while still using it for good? Those debates won't go away.

For me, the most exciting possibility is acceleration. AI won't just automate; it could help us make discoveries faster than ever. The future could be extraordinary, but only if we approach it with caution as well as curiosity.

Q46: How will AI and humans collaborate in the future?

AI Answer

The future of AI isn't humans versus machines - it's humans with machines. Collaboration will be the defining feature, reshaping how we work, learn, and create.

In workplaces, hybrid teams will become the norm. AI handles repetitive or data-heavy tasks while humans focus on strategy, empathy, and decision-making. A lawyer may rely on AI to scan thousands of cases in minutes, while focusing on building arguments. A doctor may use AI to flag anomalies in scans, while interpreting them in context and comforting the patient.

Creativity will also shift. Artists, musicians, and writers will increasingly use AI as a co-creator. Rather than replacing them, AI becomes a brainstorming partner - suggesting variations or ideas that humans refine. Some already see this as the start of a new artistic era.

Education may see teachers working alongside AI tutors. Algorithms adapt lessons to each student, while teachers bring encouragement and human connection. The collaboration could make learning both more personalized and more human.

In daily life, AI assistants will anticipate needs, manage routines, and even support mental health. The challenge will be remembering that these are tools, not companions - helpful partners, but not substitutes for relationships.

Trust will be central. For collaboration to succeed, AI must be transparent and explainable, and people must learn its strengths and limits. Training humans to "work with AI" will be just as important as technical skills.

Human Commentary

I already feel this collaboration in my own work. AI doesn't do my job for me - but it speeds me up, sharpens ideas, and sometimes even inspires me. It's like a tireless assistant who drafts, summarizes, or suggests, while I stay in charge of meaning and judgment.

When I picture the future, I don't imagine humans being replaced. I imagine those who know how to use AI working far more effectively than those who don't. Collaboration itself will be the new competitive advantage.

But there's also a cultural shift. We'll need to learn to treat AI as a partner - useful, powerful, but still just a tool. The danger is either fearing it too much or trusting it too blindly. The sweet spot is balance: respecting its capabilities without giving away our judgment.

For me, the most hopeful part is this: collaboration might actually make work and life more human. If AI takes over the repetitive parts, maybe we'll spend more time on creativity, empathy, and connection. That's the kind of partnership I'd like to see.

Q47: Who should control AI?

AI Answer

The question of who should control AI is one of the most urgent of our time. Unlike past technologies tied to one sector, AI touches everything - health, finance, defense, education, entertainment - making control both complex and crucial.

Right now, much development lies with private companies. Giants like Google, Microsoft, and OpenAI dominate because they have the resources and data. This concentration raises concerns: should technology with such wide-reaching consequences be shaped mainly by corporate interests?

Governments also play a role. Some argue national governments should regulate AI to ensure fairness and safety. The EU is already building comprehensive AI regulations, while China and the U.S. pursue their own paths. But AI is global, and national rules risk clashing or creating uneven standards.

That leads to calls for international cooperation. Some suggest AI should be governed like nuclear power or climate change - through treaties and shared frameworks. This could include banning autonomous weapons, setting ethical guidelines, and ensuring developing nations have fair access to AI tools.

Finally, there's the role of citizens. AI isn't just technical; it affects people's privacy, jobs, and freedoms. That means society should have a say. Without democratic input, AI risks being shaped by only a small elite.

The reality is that no single group should control AI. The future will require balance: companies to innovate, governments to regulate, international bodies to coordinate, and citizens to hold them all accountable. Without that balance, AI risks becoming a tool of the few instead of a benefit for the many.

Human Commentary

Whenever I hear the question "Who controls AI?", my first thought is: right now, it's mostly big tech. They have the talent, the data, and the resources. But should they be the ones deciding how AI shapes our future? I'm not convinced.

For me, AI is too important to leave in the hands of only a few corporations or governments. It influences our work, our information, even our choices. If control is too concentrated, it risks becoming a tool of power rather than a shared benefit.

I don't think there's a perfect answer. But I do think there has to be balance: governments setting boundaries, companies innovating responsibly, international agreements where possible, and people like us pushing for accountability.

The word I keep coming back to is accountability. Whoever shapes AI must answer to the public - because in the end, it touches everyone's life, not just those building it.

Q48: What role will ethics play in AI's future?

AI Answer

Ethics will sit at the center of AI's future. Unlike traditional tools, AI doesn't just follow commands - it learns, adapts, and influences human decisions. That means the impact of AI is never neutral. How we design and govern these systems will shape society for decades.

First, ethics guides design. Developers face choices about what data to include, how to handle bias, and how transparent systems should be. Without ethical principles, AI could easily become opaque - systems that make decisions no one can fully explain or challenge.

Second, ethics shapes governance. Policymakers must decide where AI is acceptable and where it's not. Should AI be allowed in policing? In warfare? In medical diagnoses? Ethical debate draws the boundaries.

Third, ethics matters in deployment. The same technology can be used for good or harm. A facial recognition tool might help find missing children - or enable mass surveillance. The difference lies not in the code, but in the ethical choices behind its use.

Looking ahead, ethics will likely be built into AI from the start. Companies and governments are already creating ethics boards and publishing guidelines. Universities now train future engineers not just in algorithms, but also in philosophy and responsibility.

But ethics isn't just for experts. Citizens also need to engage. Public debate will determine what kind of AI future we build, and whose values guide it. Ethics isn't a technical add-on - it's the compass for ensuring AI reflects human priorities.

Human Commentary

For me, the word "ethics" can sound abstract - but with AI, it's very practical. It's the difference between a system that helps and one that harms.

What I notice is how fast AI moves. New tools appear almost overnight, often without much thought about consequences. That's why I believe ethics can't come afterward - it must be baked in from the beginning.

The harder part is that ethics isn't universal. What feels acceptable in one country may feel like a violation in another. Some societies prioritize safety and control, while others prioritize freedom and privacy. Whose ethics decide? That's a tough but unavoidable question.

For me, ethics is a speed bump. It doesn't stop progress, but it forces us to slow down just enough to ask: not only "can we build this?" but also "should we?" If AI makes us pause for those conversations, maybe that's one of its hidden benefits.

Q49: How can we make sure AI stays aligned with human values?

AI Answer

Ensuring AI stays aligned with human values is one of the most urgent challenges for the future. Alignment means that systems act in ways that reflect human goals and ethics - not just what is technically efficient.

On the technical side, researchers are working on alignment methods. These include explainable AI (systems that can show why they made a decision), bias monitoring, and carefully designed reward systems that steer AI toward desirable behavior.

Governance also plays a role. Laws, standards, and international agreements will help set boundaries for what AI can and cannot do. Without regulation, alignment risks being left only to private companies, which may prioritize profit over fairness.

But there's a deeper problem: whose values? Human societies don't agree on ethics. One culture might prize privacy, another security. Some value equality above all; others prioritize freedom. Aligning AI with "human values" means negotiating these differences.

Looking ahead, the challenge grows if AI systems become more autonomous or self-improving. Experts stress building safety mechanisms now - explainability, oversight, and human-in-the-loop design - before the technology outpaces our ability to guide it.

Ultimately, alignment isn't just technical - it's social. Engineers, policymakers, and citizens all need a voice in deciding how AI reflects our values. The process won't be perfect, but without it, AI risks becoming powerful yet disconnected from what people actually want.

Human Commentary

When I hear "AI alignment", it sounds like a research problem. But to me, it's really a trust problem: can we be sure these systems act in ways we actually want?

What makes it tricky is that even humans don't fully agree on values. My priorities may be very different from someone else's, even within the same country. So, I see alignment less as "solving" values and more as constantly debating and renegotiating them.

What gives me some optimism is that alignment is already on the agenda. Researchers, companies, and governments are talking about it. But I also know how messy it is to move from principles to practice. Values shift over time, and AI will have to adapt without losing sight of its purpose.

For me, the key is making alignment a shared responsibility, not just a technical one. If only a handful of engineers or corporations decide what values are "built in", we may not like the result. But if alignment is debated openly, it can reflect society as a whole. That process won't be easy - but it's the only way I can see AI staying truly human-centered.

Q50: What's the best way for humans to prepare for an AI-driven world?

AI Answer

Preparing for an AI-driven world isn't about learning every algorithm - it's about building the skills, mindsets, and systems that let us thrive alongside intelligent machines.

The first step is AI literacy. Just as digital literacy became essential in the internet era, understanding AI will be crucial in the coming decades. This doesn't mean everyone must code neural networks, but people will need to know what AI can and cannot do, why bias matters, and when human oversight is essential. A basic grasp of AI will become as normal as knowing how to use email or spreadsheets today.

Second is adaptability. AI will continue to transform work, but it won't erase the need for human skills. Creativity, empathy, collaboration, and critical thinking remain uniquely human strengths. The most valuable workers will be those who can combine these qualities with AI tools - using machines as partners rather than competitors.

Third is lifelong learning. The pace of change means education can't end at graduation. Reskilling will become a constant part of life, whether through formal programs, workplace training, or self-guided learning. Societies that embrace continuous learning will adapt more smoothly than those that treat education as a one-time event.

On a societal level, preparation means participation. AI is too powerful to be left only to experts or corporations. Citizens need to stay engaged in debates about ethics, regulation, and governance. The shape of the AI future will depend not only on engineers and policymakers, but on the collective voice of society.

Finally, preparation has a personal dimension: cultivating curiosity over fear. Fear can paralyze, while curiosity drives exploration. By experimenting with AI tools, noticing both their strengths and limits, people can stay empowered rather than overwhelmed.

In short, the best preparation is a blend of knowledge, adaptability, and engagement. Those who approach AI as a partner - while keeping human judgment at the center - will not only survive the transition but help shape it.

Human Commentary

Preparing for an AI-shaped future isn't about learning to code or racing machines at their own game. It's about learning to adapt when the ground shifts under us. The skills that matter most may be the ones that keep us agile: asking better questions, spotting patterns, knowing when to trust the output and when to challenge it.

In my own work, I've noticed that AI doesn't erase what I do - it stretches it. It handles the routine so I can focus on judgment. It suggests ideas I hadn't considered, and I decide which ones are worth keeping. That back-and-forth feels less like rivalry and more like a new form of teamwork.

But preparation isn't only about skills. It's also about posture. If we treat AI as an enemy, we miss its potential. If we treat it as an oracle, we give away our agency. Somewhere between fear and awe lies a steadier stance: curious, questioning, willing to explore but unwilling to surrender.

And perhaps the deepest preparation has little to do with technology at all. It's about protecting the parts of us that no machine can supply - our empathy, our imagination, our sense of meaning. Those aren't side notes; they're the compass. If we hold on to them, we'll know where to place AI in our lives rather than the other way around.

Bonus Chapter: Generative AI – The New Frontier

Generative AI deserves its own chapter, because unlike other branches of artificial intelligence, it suddenly placed powerful creative tools directly in the hands of ordinary people. While earlier AI mostly worked in the background - optimizing logistics, scanning medical images, or recommending movies - generative AI puts creation itself on the table. With just a few words, anyone can produce text, images, music, code, or even video that looks like it came from a professional.

Unlike traditional AI, which recognized patterns or made predictions, generative AI produces something entirely new. It doesn't just identify an existing photo of a mountain - it can generate a picture of a mountain landscape that no camera has ever captured. This shift is not only technological but cultural: AI has moved from labs and corporations into everyday life, changing how people think about creativity, productivity, and even authorship.

The foundations stretch back decades, but only recently did computing power and training techniques make it possible at scale. Large Language Models (LLMs) learned to generate essays, stories, and code by training on billions of words. Diffusion models, starting from random digital noise, learned to generate realistic images from prompts. These breakthroughs gave us tools like ChatGPT, DALL·E, Stable Diffusion, GitHub Copilot, and others that have become household names almost overnight.

This sets the stage for the rest of the chapter. To keep things consistent with the book, each section will alternate between an AI-style explanation and my own reflections - two perspectives on the same topic.

How Generative AI Works

At its core, generative AI learns patterns from massive amounts of data and then uses those patterns to create new outputs.

For text, Large Language Models (LLMs) like GPT are trained to predict the next word in a sequence - but at a scale of billions of examples. This is why ChatGPT can write an email, a story, or a legal summary: it has absorbed the structures of language from across the internet.

For images, diffusion models start with random digital "static" and gradually refine it, step by step, until it resembles the description in your prompt. It's a bit like a sculptor chiseling away at marble until the figure emerges.

What makes these systems powerful is not raw accuracy but creative recombination. They don't copy existing material; they remix learned patterns into something new. If you ask for "a panda surfing a wave at sunset", the AI fuses elements from countless examples to produce an image no one has seen before.

Real-World Applications

Generative AI isn't just a lab experiment - it's already transforming daily life and entire industries. What makes it unique is that it's not limited to specialists: anyone can use it, from students to CEOs. Some of the most common applications include:

- Writing & Communication: Drafting emails, summarizing documents, translating languages, even ghostwriting books.
- Software Development: Tools like GitHub Copilot suggest lines of code, speed up debugging, and help beginners learn programming.
- Education: AI tutors adapt explanations to each student's level, generate practice problems, and provide instant feedback.
- Art & Design: Generating concept art, storyboards, product prototypes, or visuals for marketing campaigns in minutes.

- Healthcare: Proposing new molecular structures for drug discovery or generating synthetic medical data to train other AIs safely.
- Business & Marketing: Automating customer service chatbots, generating social media posts, and producing personalized advertising.
- Small Businesses & Startups: A café owner can now generate posters, write social media posts, and design a menu in a single afternoon - something that once required hiring multiple specialists.
- Entertainment & Media: Assisting musicians with melodies, filmmakers with storyboards, and game developers with immersive environments.

Generative AI takes tasks that once required years of training or large budgets and puts them in reach of anyone with a laptop or phone. That's why its impact feels so immediate: it lowers the barrier between an idea and its expression, turning ordinary people into creators.

Why It Matters

Generative AI is more than a clever tool - it's a shift in how humans create, work, and share ideas. Some compare it to the printing press or the internet because it doesn't just improve one field; it reshapes society. Its importance comes down to three main points:

- Democratization of creativity: Anyone can now draft an essay, design visuals, or prototype an idea without years of training.
- Acceleration of productivity: What used to take days or weeks - like writing reports, designing graphics, or testing code - can now happen in minutes.
- Redefinition of human roles: As machines take over more of the repetitive production, human work shifts toward guiding, curating, and refining what AI produces.

This combination explains both the excitement and the anxiety around generative AI. On one hand, it makes knowledge and creativity more inclusive than ever. On the other, it forces us to rethink originality, authorship, and what it means to truly "create".

The Big Debates

Generative AI is powerful, but it also raises some of the toughest questions in technology today. The main debates focus on four areas:

- Copyright & Intellectual Property: Artists and writers argue that training models on their work without consent or payment amounts to exploitation. Courts are now testing whether AI-generated works can even qualify for copyright.
- Deepfakes & Trust: Generative AI can create videos or voices that are almost impossible to distinguish from reality. This risks fueling misinformation, scams, and the erosion of trust in what we see and hear.
- Bias & Fairness: Since AI reflects the data it learns from, it can reproduce stereotypes or inequalities - sometimes subtly, sometimes blatantly. Without safeguards, this could reinforce existing problems rather than solve them.
- Overreliance: If students rely on AI to write essays or professionals lean on it for decisions, we risk losing core skills like critical thinking, creativity, and judgment. The danger isn't just mistakes - it's forgetting how to think for ourselves.

These are not just technical issues. They touch culture, ethics, and politics. How we answer them will determine whether generative AI becomes a tool that empowers people - or one that deepens problems.

What's Next?

Generative AI is still in its early days, and the next steps could be even more transformative. A few trends stand out:

- Multimodality: Future systems won't just handle text or images separately - they'll combine them. You might describe: "A short video of a sunrise over Copenhagen with gentle background music", and the AI could generate the whole thing at once: script, visuals, soundtrack, narration.

- Personalization: Instead of generic tools, people may train their own AI on their personal data - emails, notes, calendars, and preferences. These "digital twins" could act in your style, anticipate your needs, and even filter information on your behalf.

- Integration into daily life: Generative AI will likely fade into the background, powering apps, devices, and services without us even thinking about it. It may become as ordinary - and invisible - as electricity or the internet.

- Unpredictable breakthroughs: Perhaps the most important point: no one really knows where it's heading. The pace is so fast that applications we can't imagine today may appear in just a few years.

The only certainty is that generative AI won't fade away. It will evolve, spread, and continue to reshape how we work, learn, and create. The challenge - and the opportunity - will be learning to guide it wisely.

Human Commentary

One of the first times I tried generative AI, I asked it to create a description of a futuristic café in Helsinki, complete with a menu and atmosphere. Within seconds, it gave me something that felt like a travel brochure for a place that didn't exist. My reaction was half awe, half disbelief. Was this creativity? Was it mine, or the AI's? Or just a collage of borrowed fragments?

At work, I've asked ChatGPT to analyze data, draft pitches, or even role-play as a skeptical client before a meeting. Sometimes it's brilliant. Sometimes it makes silly mistakes. But it always saves me time and sparks new ideas.

In personal life, I've used it for planning trips, suggesting workouts, and testing recipes. It's helpful - though I'd still trust my grandmother's cooking over anything an algorithm suggests.

That's the paradox of generative AI: it feels like magic, but it's really math. A tool that can amaze and frustrate in the same moment.

If someone asked me at dinner what it really is, I'd say: "It's the technology that put AI in everyone's hands. It lets anyone create, but it also reflects our culture back at us - the good and the bad. What we see in it depends a lot on what we bring to it".

That's what I keep coming back to. Generative AI feels magical, but it's also a reflection of us - our culture, our data, our choices. Whether it empowers or overwhelms depends less on the technology and more on us - the same message that runs through this whole book.

Final Thoughts: What We've Learned, and What Lies Ahead

After exploring the rise of generative AI and its unique impact, it's time to take a step back and reflect on the bigger picture: what we've learned from this journey, what remains uncertain, and how this knowledge might guide us in the years to come.

Over the course of fifty questions and fifty answers, we've seen AI explained by the machine itself - and then reframed through a human lens. That dialogue has shown us not just what AI can do, but also what it cannot, and perhaps more importantly, what it reveals about us.

AI, at its heart, is about patterns. It does not think like us, feel like us, or dream like us. It predicts, classifies, and generates based on probabilities. And yet, because it operates at a scale far beyond human capacity, it can appear astonishingly intelligent - even creative. This tension, between what AI is and what it seems to be, is central to understanding its role in our world.

Key Takeaways from the Journey

1. AI Basics

We've learned that AI is not magic. It's data-driven, pattern-based, and built on algorithms that find structure where humans might see noise. Understanding this helps demystify the hype: AI isn't a mind, but a tool. Recognizing that difference is the first step to using it wisely.

2. AI in Action

From chatbots that mimic conversation to medical systems that detect cancerous cells, AI's applications are both broad and impactful. It thrives in environments where massive amounts of data can be analyzed quickly, making it indispensable in fields like healthcare, finance, and logistics - but also surprisingly useful in everyday tasks like organizing your inbox or helping you choose the fastest route to work.

3. Risks & Ethics

We've seen that AI's strengths can also be its weaknesses. Bias in training data can perpetuate unfairness. Overreliance on automated systems can dull human judgment. And without thoughtful regulation, AI can be misused for misinformation, surveillance, or manipulation. These are not problems for the distant future - they are challenges we face right now.

4. Philosophy & the Future

Finally, AI invites us to ask bigger questions: What does it mean to be creative? To make decisions? To be human? As machines begin to mimic more aspects of human thought, we are challenged to define what truly sets us apart - and perhaps even to rediscover the value of our humanity in sharper focus.

Practical Lessons: AI in Everyday Life

The easiest way to see AI's value is to picture it in ordinary lives.

Take a high school teacher overwhelmed with grading essays. With AI, she can generate personalized lesson plans, create quiz questions in minutes, and adapt material to different student levels. Does this replace her? No. It frees her to focus on what matters most: teaching, mentoring, and inspiring her students.

Think about a small café owner. Ten years ago, AI was irrelevant to her daily work. Today, she can use it to design seasonal menus, generate promotional images for Instagram, or create engaging loyalty campaigns that attract repeat customers. The technology doesn't replace her - it amplifies her creativity and helps her connect with customers.

Or imagine a doctor in a rural clinic. He doesn't have access to the same equipment as a major hospital, but with AI diagnostic tools, he can catch rare diseases or unusual conditions that might otherwise be missed. AI doesn't replace his judgment - it acts like a diagnostic assistant, giving him additional confidence in his decisions.

Consider a student preparing for exams. Instead of flipping endlessly through textbooks, she uses AI tutors that adjust study schedules, generate practice problems, and even quiz her in interactive ways. Here AI isn't a shortcut to avoid learning, but a coach that makes study more personal and adaptive.

Even a retiree might benefit. Picture someone curious about learning a new language at 70. With AI-powered apps, lessons become interactive, encouraging, and fun - turning what might have felt intimidating into a joyful experience.

The best use of AI isn't about machines taking over, but about humans and machines working together, each doing what they do best.

What We Still Need to Learn

Of course, the journey is far from over. There are pressing questions still unanswered, and each comes with its own risks if left unaddressed.

Can we build truly explainable AI?

Right now, many systems are "black boxes" - we know what they output, but not always why. Imagine being denied a bank loan and no one, not even the bank manager, can tell you why. That kind of opacity undermines trust. Creating transparent systems is essential if AI is to be accepted fairly.

How do we regulate AI without stifling innovation? Governments are scrambling to write rules, but the technology evolves faster than the law. AI faces the same challenge as the early internet: opportunity racing ahead of rules. We'll need smart, flexible regulation that protects people without freezing progress.

What happens to work?

Some jobs will vanish, others will be transformed, and entirely new ones will appear. But what about the transition period? If millions of workers are displaced before new opportunities arrive, societies could face instability. Preparing people with retraining, social safety nets, and cultural readiness will be as important as the technology itself.

Will AI ever approach consciousness?

It's a philosophical question as much as a technical one - and perhaps the most intriguing mystery of all. If a machine convincingly seems conscious, how should we treat it? And what would that say about our own definitions of life, mind, and meaning?

A Final Word

When I began writing this book, I was curious: could AI really explain itself? Could it answer our questions clearly and honestly? What I discovered is that AI can help, but it cannot replace the human effort of shaping, questioning, and guiding the answers. Even this book - partly drafted with AI - didn't "write itself". It took time, energy, and many revisions to turn raw material into something coherent and meaningful.

That, in the end, is the true lesson of this experiment: AI can provide answers, but meaning comes from the human side of the dialogue. The questions we ask - and the values we bring to them - matter just as much as the answers we receive.

So use this knowledge wisely. Question boldly. Create responsibly. And remember: AI isn't just the future. It's already here. The real story begins now - with us.

Thank You to the Reader

Writing this book has been a journey, not just into the world of artificial intelligence, but also into how we, as humans, try to understand and adapt to change. If you've read this far, it means you've shared that journey with me - and for that, I'm deeply grateful.

I hope these pages gave you more than just definitions and explanations. I hope they sparked curiosity, provoked new questions, and maybe even made you smile in a few places. AI is complex, but learning about it doesn't have to feel heavy. My goal was to make it approachable - something you can talk about at work, with friends, or even at the dinner table.

Above all, thank you for your time and attention. In a world of constant distraction, choosing to spend it on a book - even one shaped in part by AI - means a lot to me.

This book is just a starting point. AI will keep changing, and so will the conversations around it. I encourage you to keep exploring, questioning, and above all, keeping the human perspective at the center.

- Stephen D. Carver

Printed in Dunstable, United Kingdom

70533806R00072